Forecasting Tomorrow: The Future of Safety Excellence

Shawn M. Galloway & Terry L. Mathis

Published by SCE Press

Cover design by Leigh Anne Griffin

ISBN 978-0692460580

For our family

Thank you for your love, support and encouragement.

Contents

Introduction

Safety is rarely viewed as an exciting or interesting discussion topic for business leaders. Too often, safety is something delegated, outsourced, and, if we are honest, typically only thought of with great concern when bad things occur. With the exception of being viewed as a cost-center to manage, safety has not been regarded as a strategic value-contributor to organizations, and it's no wonder.

Few business excellence books or university teachings mention direction of safety improvement efforts other than injury rates, legal responsibility, and how to mitigate operational, personal and process risk. "Fail less!" is the rallying cry, haphazard and meaningless goals of zero something-or-another abound.

Even with good intent, efforts to prevent injuries often disengage, distract and demotivate the very individuals whose discretionary effort is needed in order to significantly improve. Zero injuries is no longer the challenge for the best of the best. Rather, it is knowing precisely how it was achieved and how it can be sustained through creating want-to rather than have-to cultures, while maintaining the mindset that even great results can always be better.

Thankfully, times are changing.

Emerging trends are becoming increasing visible among multi-industries regarding how safety is viewed, thought of, strategically managed, and how progress is measured. Moreover, the cast of characters, the roles they play, and accountability for behavioral responsibilities are evolving, all for the better. While a plethora of companies have a long way to go on the journey to safety excellence, certain companies are leading the pack.

As we partner with this range of companies we see these trends and use our observations in the articles we publish monthly. A number of these articles have been compiled and included to support these predictions of future trends in safety.

In the following pages, we will share with you our predictions of where safety efforts will be heading over the next several years. Such knowledge can help you to strategically plan for safety success in the future.

Foreword

Looking out over the city of Baku, Azerbaijan while running on a treadmill made in China, listening to a TED talk led by a gentlemen from Switzerland, playing on a device conceived by a company in California, contemplating the leadership keynote I was to give later that day, I finally landed on my personal mission.

Throughout my professional career, I have always had a passion for excellence in everything I do due to the work ethics instilled in me by my parents when I was a young, first-time employee. I've been honored to be recognized for my work, but I've continued to struggle with succinctly verbalizing my personal mission. It finally became clear.

Running at a moderate pace, I quickly grabbed the handrails of the treadmill and diverted my feet to the adjoining sides of the moving belt. I had it. My mission is to continuously challenge and evolve the global thinking around safety excellence. Knowing everyone is at a different level of maturity in the journey to safety excellence, I know I need to sometimes start with an even more basic definition: What is the real goal of safety?

Challenging the Goal of Safety

Having delivered the introductory keynote speech at the first ever International Safety Conference in the country of Azerbaijan, I'm feeling confident the global views of safety are evolving. Following established government Environmental, Health and Safety (EHS) regulations, the safety requirements of customers is now being viewed as the minimal necessary rather than the final destination. A healthy, new debate is emerging. What is the goal in safety?

Many organizations set their goal as a reduction rate, such as 20 percent improvement year over year. Others express their goal as ensuring employees leave their jobs at the end of their work day injury-free or "zero injuries". More and more businesses are recognizing employees are often more exposed to risk outside of the workplace, and have evolved the goal to include employees also returning to work injury-free. But if we achieve a day, month or year injury-free, have we truly reached our goal? Did we accomplish this by being safer or just luckier this year?

Performing an online search for "the goal of safety" at the time of this writing, over 760,000 links resulted, with many differing views. Articles abound in which safety consultants write about their belief that zero incidents is the ultimate goal of safety. I strongly disagree. Incidents are failures in the established EHS management systems. It is doubtful that the systems were created to expect defects. When an incident occurs, someone has found a flaw in the system. Is the ultimate goal truly only to have no failures?

Aside from the demotivated culture you create (work hard to fail less), this goal can actually encourage risk-taking. If no injuries is equivalent to "safe" or "safety excellence", it is logical for the workforce to develop a dangerous perception that, "Anything I do that does not result in an injury must be safe and what the company wants!"

This thinking is just as dangerous as assuming your state of health is perfect because you have no recognizable illness or disease. Is the ultimate goal of safety the absence of incidents or injuries? No!

Author Marty Rubin once wrote, "When the meaning is unclear, there is no meaning." In establishing or improving existing transformative goals, it is vital the leader begins their path not by looking for the next improvement opportunity, but instead with the clarity of knowing what the terms "safe", "safety", "at-risk" and "safety excellence" mean. Without clarity, efforts will be disjointed, misaligned, minimally supported and potentially demotivating.

To assist in creating this clarity, answer the following questions independently, and then with input from others.

1. What does "safe" mean?
2. How would you define "safety"?
3. What is acceptable and necessary risk?
4. What is unacceptable and unnecessary risk?
5. What would you see and hear if "zero incidents" was achieved?
6. What is "safety excellence"?

Safety must be defined and measured by what we collectively do to reduce risk exposure and by what you want, rather than solely by outcomes or undesirable results. Organizations that believe they have achieved excellence in safety performance and culture because they have not experienced failures are often the same ones surprised by a major catastrophe or a series of unfortunate events. We should not allow ourselves to narrowly define safety excellence by what we know as excellent practices, measurements, and cultures of today. For what is perceived as great in safety now will later be looked at in a similar appalling manner as how we view practices of just twenty years ago.

I have personally dedicated my life to a single, yet recognizably complex, mission: to continuously challenge and evolve the global thinking around safety excellence. I am fortunate the passion for my work has attracted many of the best in safety in every major industry. With every engagement, even my own thinking expands and prompts me to question what I believed about safety excellence when I awoke in the morning. When we believe we know all there is to know about any subject, we not only do an injustice to ourselves, but also to those we impact with the goals we establish and the language we use to achieve them.

– Shawn M. Galloway
July 2015

Like Shawn, I have dedicated my life's work to the continuous improvement of safety. I began safety improvement efforts first in my corporate career, then carried it outside to the rest of the world. It began with a few techniques I learned and shared, and has expanded significantly over the past two decades into true thought leadership and innovation. I don't claim full credit for this exponential growth, as much of it was learned on client locations through extensive experimentation and in seeking better methodologies.

I am still a bit awed by the synergy created between consultant and client on such projects. If done in the right spirit, such collaboration multiplies greatly the creative thinking of both parties and gives them both a laboratory in which to test their ideas.

Even these predictions for the future have been greatly influenced by our clients. It is, after all, their futures we are predicting as well as our own. Seeing what is important to them helps draw the line from where we are to where we want to be, and it is somewhere on or near that line where we will find the future. The realizations of these past years has greatly shaped that future. Basic thinking in safety is giving way to more advanced concepts, and accepted practices are being questioned, and often replaced.

Likewise, my collaboration with Shawn Galloway has greatly expanded my range of thinking. It is rare to find another individual who is similar enough in thinking to truly work well together, yet different enough to add new value and perspective. Shawn is such an individual. He is willing to challenge ideas if he thinks they are flawed but also able to see kernels of good thought in many ideas that are worth utilizing and expanding. All his efforts have been forward thinking rather than resistant or pushing back. This kind of idea expansion has made us both more effective consultants, partners, and thought leaders.

Safety has been and will be even more influenced by forces outside its boundaries. In the past two decades, the outside influences have been largely academic. Psychology, sociology, and the behavioral sciences have attempted to turn their sciences into technologies useful in safety improvement. In the future, outside influences will be more strategic and business oriented. Safety will become more of a core business area rather than a delegated or outsourced specialty. The dichotomous idea of productivity versus safety will give way to a true concept of safe work.

Many of the accepted and heritage activities of safety will be tested for effectiveness, and many will fail. The "more is better" mentality will give way to improving the quality rather than the quantity of safety activities. Safety will be truly improved rather than simply added to.

All predictions are necessarily based on current thinking and trends. Any outstanding innovations or changes in the future can re-route the direction safety is taking. But we feel confident these main core directions are firmly entrenched into the current thinking of organizational leaders, and that thinking will steer safety efforts in these directions barring any huge interference in this path. Leaders can benefit greatly from glimpsing the future through the eyes of other leaders. It is for this reason and the others mentioned above that I think this book can add great value to both current and future safety efforts.

-Terry L. Mathis
July 2015

Prediction #1: Excellence Reframed

Strategy and methodology will be the defining qualities of excellence rather than lagging indicators. We will realize the lack of accidents does not completely define excellence and good performance can always be better. Excellence will be defined as the profound knowledge of how lagging indicators are impacted and the ability to repeat excellent results.

The Mindset of Safety Excellence

There are sites I'm scared to visit — sites where everyone believes they are excellent in safety performance and culture. Our thoughts, the language we use and how they complement or conflict with our behavior will affect our ability to improve safety. When we believe we are excellent in safety, we tend to stop looking to improve. When we say all incidents can be prevented, yet we track non-preventable vehicle incidents, we create confusion and disbelief in the objectives. We strive for excellence in all we do in safety. The problem develops when we believe we have already achieved it.

In early 1900s America, the industry estimates for construction fatalities on skyscrapers was one death per floor built. Now, we wouldn't conceive of such evaluations. In many industries, the safety practices as recent as 10 years ago are no longer acceptable. Working with several clients employing meter readers, I found the long-accepted practice of fence jumping to obtain readings is becoming culturally viewed as unacceptable. Yet, it takes time to change long-term, strongly-held and reinforced beliefs and behaviors. Culture change is a transformation and a transformation is a process, not a program or an event.

9

Some client organizations have adopted the term "Better Practice" to replace "Best Practice". They believe when a best practice is adopted, employees will stop looking for a better way and fall into the confirmation bias trap, only favoring information confirming the chosen path is still best. It is easy to fall in love with a methodology, and many individuals' careers rest on its continued success, persuading continued investment even when it is no longer yielding value.

Preparing to deliver the keynote at a Cintas Corp. private conference, I learned a lot about the organization and its values. Cintas strives to embody a sense of positive discontent in all individuals and decisions. Author, Mark Sanborn, notes positive discontent is similar to "better rather than best-practice" thinking:

> "Positive discontent is the combination of gratitude and discontent. It doesn't discount or diminish what we've been able to accomplish, but neither does it allow us to rest on our laurels. Positive discontent allows us to enjoy what we've achieved without the attendant danger of becoming complacent."

The most effective safety effort is neither blind to the magnitude of the challenge nor resigned to accept some level of failure. Likewise, the most effective safety effort is always intelligently adapting but never knee-jerk reacting. Where the idealist would fail to adapt and the realist overreact, the effective safety professional continuously analyzes and improves the approach, always looking for the next better way to improve safety. It is possible to dream the impossible dream without tilting at windmills.

Safety excellence is a journey that never ends. We should celebrate our successes when the results improve and have a sense of confidence in their continuance, especially when we know what led to improvement. We should celebrate when we see the culture evolving and positively shaping the beliefs and behaviors of new members and contractors. We should always remember, however, that all risks can never be completely removed from any industrial setting. Moreover, we should remember our employees are most likely to be injured away from work. We will continue to make progress when there is pride in what has been accomplished, yet a healthy sense of vulnerability remains. Everyone within the organization must realize, "Sure we are good; but there will always be a better way."

The Only Way Safety Will Continuously Improve

All progress begins by thinking differently. If we seek different results, we must ask more intelligent questions and realize today's answers will be antiquated tomorrow. What questions are you asking? Do you allow the status quo to remain unchallenged?

When the first skyscraper, the Tacoma Building, was constructed in Chicago in 1889, walking on steel beams high in the air without any protection from falling was the only way to complete the work. As stated previously, fatalities became so common in the construction of multi-level buildings that insurance adjustors would anticipate one death per floor constructed.

In 1927, the inventors of the bulletproof vest would demonstrate the quality and assurances of their work by firing live rounds, not at a mannequin, but at a live person. Confidence in product to secure sales took precedence over safety. This was viewed not only as acceptable, but impressive, and it built a community of customer confidence in the manufacturer's brand.

In March of 1923, a patent was granted to Emma Read of Spokane, Washington for a cage to hold a baby which could be, according to the patent, "suspended upon the exterior of a building adjacent an open window, wherein the baby or young child may be placed." Finally getting traction in 1937 as more and more individuals left rural areas and moved into cities, one group in London, the Chelsea Baby Club, saw the health risk the patented device could overcome and issued their members these cages.

With the change from farmhouse living to city dwellings, this group of well-intending individuals were concerned that infants and toddlers were not getting adequate oxygen and sun exposure, so open-air steel cages were built and affixed to the exterior of buildings, often several floors above street-level, for the children to "play" in. Again, with good intentions, this was viewed not only as acceptable, but was perceived to contribute to a healthier child.

Since their inception, personnel working for electric and gas distribution companies were often required to climb over fences in order to access meters for billing purposes. Dog bites and confrontations with angry customers became common. Many of these companies are now installing automated meter reading (AMRs) devices to negate the need to access a backyard. Moreover, these organizations are working to change the perceptions of these hard working meter readers to believe it is no longer necessary or acceptable to "hop the fence." It is now considered an unnecessary risk by leadership. What are the employee-perceived acceptable and unacceptable risks in your organization? How well do they align with management's perception of acceptable and unacceptable risks? Where does the documentation of this great insight exist in your organization? How regularly is it updated and improved? What experiences are hindering or progressing the lowering of risk-tolerance?

An energy exploration client, working aggressively to control and influence the behaviors (mandatory and discretionary) of their drilling contractors, engaged us over several years to help align their primary contractor cultures with their own. Visiting the various operating areas, the lead people onsite could all share an experience they had with the visiting Executive Vice President. When time pressure situations were discussed, they all heard him state, "The oil has been in the ground for millions of years; it can wait another day. We don't need to go so fast that it compromises safety."

While this was admirable and attempted to reinforce safety values, several times that same day, engineering would call these same onsite leaders who had heard the EVP's message to see how much progress had been made (how many stages had been completed). Sometimes to make progress, the right question isn't, "What do we need to do?" The question is often, "What do we need to stop doing?" or, "What are we doing that is sending the wrong message?"

We have come a long way in safety and will continue to make strides when executive leaders are aligned with the importance of integrating safety thinking into business decisions. Now, more than ever before, if we want everyone to be on the same page regarding the direction of the organization and the role safety plays, we need to discuss and document what is acceptable and unacceptable risk and close the gaps that might exist.

Similar to what we outlined in *STEPS to Safety Culture Excellence*^{SM}, organizational clarity is vital. If we believe excellence is defined with antiquated beliefs, we will continue to get the same results. As we move into the next decade of safety improvement efforts, we predict there will be increasing language, methodology and effort focused on redefining what excellence means to safety performance and culture.

Excellence isn't just great results; it is the ability to repeat the results, know precisely how they were achieved, and always recognize opportunities where the system could be better. How do you define excellence in safety? Most importantly, how do others within your organization define it, and is this helping or hindering your progress towards continuous improvement?

Government Will Evolve Focus

Regulators and government agencies will increase focus on culture and personal accountability. They will look for cultural influences underlying deaths and disasters and for personal, as well as organizational, responsibility.

The foundation for this thinking was laid in the congressional intervention with NASA after the Challenger disaster. Failing to find an adequate scapegoat, congress and OSHA cited a poor safety culture and lack of accountability as the culprits. They put outside industrial leaders on NASA's advisory board to purportedly help them correct these problems.

The United Kingdom recently took this thinking to almost ridiculous lengths by blaming business leaders and organizations for virtually every accident that occurred. A change in administrations and some highly-publicized absurdities have reversed this trend to a large part, but the tendency toward a focus on culture and accountability were revealed.

China has actually executed some organizational executives for safety infractions, but they have also done so for fraud, which questions whether accountability is strictly driven by safety considerations.

Here in the USA, some executives have been charged with various indictments for safety disasters and some have even served jail time when convicted.

We believe personal accountability will continue to become a focus for government agencies with an emphasis initially on leaders. When leaders influence workers to take safety shortcuts or fail to provide what is needed to do jobs safely, they will be held more and more personally accountable. This thinking will begin to expand to the worker level as well, with workers being held more accountable for their own performance mostly in relation to compliance issues.

Personal accountability for safety will be seen as a building block of safety culture. First, make strong individuals and build them into strong teams. Then create an overall culture in which safety practices are consistent and interpersonally reinforced. Such cultures will be viewed as critical elements for safety excellence and sustainability in organizations.

OSHA's Voluntary Protection Program (VPP), which has been greatly weakened under the last administration, will likely either be scrapped in favor of another initiative to promote safety culture or will be re-focused to become the vehicle for promoting culture and personal accountability, rather than just participation.

Organizations already working on culture and accountability may be able to influence regulators and legislators by showing them successful models and metrics. Government has a sense of direction but not a detailed vision of what success might look like. Industries who successfully blaze the trail may well influence future legislation and regulation and the metrics used for such actions.

Key Points:

- Organizations will turn from their over-reliance on lagging indicators and begin to view excellence in terms of the strategy and methodology that produce the results.

- Continuous improvement will pervade safety thinking and a degree of positive discontent will overcome the complacency created by periods of low accident rates.

- Government and regulatory agencies will become another reason for organizations to work toward excellent safety cultures and personal accountability as they focus their enforcement toward such targets.

- Individuals at all levels will begin to be held more and more accountable for their safety choices and performance.

- Personal accountability will continue to become a focus for government agencies with an emphasis initially on leaders.

- Safety culture will be more encouraged, scrutinized and regulated in the near future, but will require top-down leadership to set the path of culture change.

Prediction #2: From Programs to Strategy

Organizations will move away from programmatic and towards a strategic approach to safety. Organizations will develop overarching safety strategies and align them with business strategies, and all programs will be evaluated as to whether or not they fit and support the strategy. Leaders will no longer simply adopt programs to address problems. Strategy will drive safety efforts toward even more proactive actions and away from the reactive firefighting mentality of the past.

Science Supports but Doesn't Lead Strategy

Safety improvement methodology will become more holistic and business-based. Single science, single methodology experts will decrease in perceived long-term value.

The advent of behavior-based safety (BBS) and all its offshoots in the mid-1980s brought about the elevation of the academic scientist to the perceived level of safety expert. Managers who were stuck in command-and-control models were enamored with new possibilities to better control worker behavior or even form processes which controlled worker behavior without their intervention. It seemed the answers to improving safety had laid dormant in the fields of psychology, sociology, and the behavioral sciences. Experts in these fields were quick to bring their bag of tricks to the safety field and found it lucrative to do so.

The overall impact of this phenomena were positive. Safety management was shaken out of its comfort zone and further improvements were realized. However, the limitations of these approaches were also revealed as the processes matured and stagnated or, in some instances, failed to produce results.

The weaknesses of the one-science or single-program approach to safety came from both sides of the process. Scientists had a blind spot to the reality of business and failed to turn their pure science into elegant technology that fit the environment in which it had to be implemented. Business leaders were mystified by the science and didn't take a leading role in its implementation, which pushed safety outside the mainstream of the business. If a safety culture was created by BBS, it was a sub-culture of the true organizational culture which had other priorities and management styles.

As the safety conversation changes from behavior to culture, organizational leaders realize they need to take a more active role and rely less on single-science experts and processes. Safety culture is an aspect of company culture and cannot be delegated or outsourced. Any outside professional advisors who are asked to help improve safety culture should help organizational leaders to incorporate it rather than encouraging them to delegate it.

This view that safety is an aspect of business rather than a mysterious, touchy-feely science designed to manipulate workers into being safe is the beginning of safety culture excellence. The best safety cultures today are strategically led by business leaders, advised by business-based consultants, and integrated into the mainstream of business. Business strategies and safety strategies are developed to work synergistically rather than compete with each other. Safety and productivity are portrayed as allies rather than enemies and "safe production" is the vision of the effort.

This does not discount the role of academic scientists nor ban them from safety practices. Rather, it puts their potential contribution into business perspective and makes the utilization of their processes contingent on fit with business and safety strategy. The appeal of single-science based programs and processes is diminishing and the era of overarching strategy is emerging. And it is emerging quickly!

More is Not Better; Only Better is Better

When safety results are unsatisfactory, managers tend to say, "We are not doing enough for safety." There is an assumption that more effort will produce better results. In the short term, this often seems true. When leaders focus on one priority over others, followers tend to direct their efforts accordingly. Leaders assume that their additional activities produced the desired results. Often, it was not the effort but simply the priority that drove the improvement. Regardless of how such knee-jerk reactions work, long-term, sustainable results depend more on the quality rather than the quantity of effort.

One organization increased the hours workers spent in classroom training because they discovered knowledge deficits had contributed to accidents. Accident rates reduced but knowledge levels did not rise. The emphasis on reducing accidents had focused worker efforts, but the training had not been effective in improving knowledge. Leaders realized after some investigation that the problem was the *quality* of the training. The training did not address the most critical knowledge needed. Increasing the quantity of the poorly designed training had simply subjected workers to more meaningless and ineffective activity. When the quality of the training was improved, more quantity was not needed.

Many organizations purchase the latest fads in safety training and programs in hopes of improving results. Again, there is this assumption that more is better, rather than improving existing programs and training and aligning them with a better safety strategy. Unfortunately, "more" doesn't fix "poor".

Very few organizations are failing to dedicate enough effort to safety, but many are not using that effort to its maximum effectiveness. The answer is not more effort, but better effort.

Improving Safety: Programs vs. People

The last several times I have asked clients what they are doing to make workers safer, they answered with a list of safety programs. There is an underlying assumption that programs can shape people. While training, meetings, onboarding and communication are definitely influences on peoples' behavioral choices, they are far from the only ones. I have witnessed situations in which such programs were doing mortal battle with the workplace, the culture, production pressure and other powerful, daily factors which influenced workers to take risks. The poor programs were outnumbered and overpowered. These other influences were not being addressed in the safety efforts except through trying to strengthen the programs.

The recent emphasis and popularity of focusing on safety "culture" is, in part, an admission that people-to-people influences are important and must be addressed. However, most organizations attempt to improve the safety culture by using MORE PROGRAMS! Again, the assumption is that programs shape people and people even shape each other. Many organizations are attempting to change the seeds of culture while ignoring the climate and chemistry in which they want the seeds to grow.

What often brings success is exactly the opposite approach. People respond to the environment in which they work, which includes physical design, leadership, supervision style, respect for lifestyle issues, and being treated like an adult. For a brief moment, forget what your programs should be and focus on what your people should be. What influences will make them feel good about becoming such a person and how can you create these influences in your organization?

Checking Off the Box

When can good safety practices go bad? When they become routine and quit adding value to the daily safety of workers. In short, when they are completed just to check off the box that says they are completed. This seldom happens intentionally. Most safety programs and activities have very specific goals to increase safety awareness, provide pre-job planning, or keep safety on everyone's' mind. But when programs stress the quantity without the quality, they can become meaningless activities.

Safety moments, Job Safety Analyses, audits, observations, refresher training, and safety toolbox meetings can all add value or become valueless activities based on how they are done. As soon as any safety activity is speedily "checked off" just to get it done, there is opportunity to continue doing it this way. It is incumbent on everyone to question the value of safety efforts and not let them become meaningless. This means leaders must listen to workers regularly and keep in touch with the reality of shop-floor safety. If doing it poorly ever becomes acceptable, the die is cast. In this, as in most safety efforts, prevention is preferable to reaction.

Simply adopting more or better programs is never the right approach. Decisions on how best to improve safety must be made, based on data, determining how to capture and add value. Tradeoffs are necessary as no one can do everything.

Tradeoffs often involve abandoning activities that fail to add value. This is why strategy is crucial for the future of safety efforts. Most importantly, the strategy should support and not hinder or constrict the business strategy. How well does your safety strategy align with your business strategy? Does your new program contribute to the business efforts or make them harder to accomplish?

Safety will never become a core value within a company culture until the safety strategy supports and is aligned with the business strategy. Every organization has a "safety culture," but could it be better? Improvement is achieved by continuously doing things better, and capturing and delivering real value. How efficient and value-focused are your safety efforts?

You Need to Manage Strategically

Imagine a senior operational leader of any business who is unable to produce a strategic plan. Such inabilities would be career-limiting and characterize the individual as a doer not a thinker, or as a task-master rather than a strategist. Strategy is, in fact, what makes great operational leaders.

Much has been written about the need for safety to be integrated into business thinking if safety is to become the way of business and a core value rather than just a priority. Not enough attention is placed on the need for business practices to be integrated into safety thinking.

Safety is not simple. It is more than rule-following, common-sense and paying attention. Safety is influenced by culture, systems, leadership styles, history, economy, location, etc. With organizations of all sizes, industries, maturity of safety systems, performance and culture, one of the most significant differentiators of successful organizations in safety is the way safety is strategically managed. Consider: What is your three-to five-year strategic plan? How effectively this question is answered is the difference in tactical vs. strategic thinking.

High-Performance Businesses Seek Strategy, Not Tactics

A long-term client who is a best-in-industry organization and has a 45,000 global employee base, currently has forty open positions for qualified safety professionals to meet business growth. During a regular strategy session with senior leadership to address this very issue, a shared frustration prompted a discussion about the future for safety professionals and a plan to overcome organizational shortcomings. Universities and on-the-job company training tend to produce safety technicians rather than strategists.

Of course, we need technically-focused and program subject-matter experts. Most importantly, we need individuals who are able to challenge status-quo thinking and perceptions about what is possible, and to direct resources and prioritize initiatives to advancing performance and culture. It is the strategists that will advance safety, both in industry and individual company performance.

Safety Follows Strategy

Strategy, as a business concept, is relatively new. In fact, not until the early 1960s did the term move beyond a military or political meaning to being recognized as valuable in the business domain. "Strategy's coming to dominance as the framework by which companies understand what they're doing and want to do, the construct through which and around which the rest of their efforts are organized, eclipses any other change worked in the intellectual landscape of business over the past fifty years." (Kiechel, 2010)

In fact, in the United States, it wasn't until December 29, 1970 that President Nixon signed the Occupational Safety and Health Act of 1970 into law. Whether coincidence or following the reprioritization of government and business values, safety followed strategy in the history of business in America. Forty years later, safety in most industries and businesses have experienced a downward trend in injuries and severity due largely to the level of attention, advancements in technology, systems- and behavioral-thinking and, occasionally, brute force awareness campaigns. Safety will improve with additional attention, but will fail to produce additional return on investment without a better model to prioritize attention and energy.

Initiatives and Results are Not Strategies
Most are familiar with Albert Einstein's continuously referenced quote, "Insanity is doing the same thing over and over again and expecting different results." Yet, here we are in 2015 with the average business and safety professional looking for the next hand injury, house-keeping, behavior, severity or near-miss program. Developing an awareness campaign, improving reporting, achieving zero injuries, and obtaining OSHA VPP Star Status are all initiatives and outcomes; they are not strategies.

Strategy should be set by those with a vision, rather than those motivated by closing gaps, or by those compensated by reductions in cost or program implementations. Organizational leaders must first outline and clearly communicate what excellence looks like, where they are currently, how the journey will be taken and how measurements of progress will be recognized and communicated along the way. It is natural to first focus on the current state and then plan to close the gap. This is a mistake and is outlined in the 2013 book, *STEPS to Safety Culture Excellence*.

"It has been suggested to us many times that an assessment should be the starting place for the journey to Safety Culture Excellence rather than developing a safety strategy. In our experience, when you begin with the assessment, your strategy can become simply a plan to address your weaknesses rather than a true strategy. It is like planning your life based on a visit to your doctor's office. A strategy should give direction and meaning to everything else you do in safety."

Strategy is more than ideas, promising or provoking. It is the ability to devise a framework that allows for the continuous prioritization of decisions, resources and initiatives to accomplish and sustain business objectives (e.g., customer saturation, quality, productivity, and safety). Every organization seeks to capture as much market share as possible. For-profit companies seek to attract the largest amount of consumers. Not-for-profit groups seek both the largest amount of charitable contribution and the majority of hearts and minds. In both regards, safety is no different. Professionals position their value-add for a substantial piece of the budget, but also attempt to sway employee attention share.

The Two Focal Points of Safety Excellence Strategy
Safety goals and objectives must be focused on two areas: incident and injury prevention, and the creation of Safety Culture Excellence. Organizations must maintain a comprehensive prioritization process to determine where to focus incident and injury prevention efforts. Typically they are concentrated on conditions (e.g., work space, design, systems) and behaviors (i.e., mandatory and discretionary).

Culture is just as important, as it is the most effective sustainability mechanism. Culture is why prevention efforts succeed or fail. While culture is certainly affected by efforts to improve, they must be a fundamental and proactive part of the strategy to ensure acceptance, alignment and sustainability. Consider discussing with other operational leaders to identify and map out the following:

- What does Safety Culture Excellence look like? (Think observed performance, not just results)
- If we had 100% acceptance with rules, policies and procedures, what other effort is needed to ensure incident-free performance?
- If we achieved incident-free performance and were asked to describe the reason, what is our response?
- What would the common beliefs be that reinforce the reason we have achieved excellence in performance and culture? (Identify the top 3 beliefs.)
- What experiences would be occurring consistently to reinforce these beliefs?
- What are the leadership safety roles, responsibilities to ensure these experiences are occurring?

There are many questions this should prompt. For the evolution of thinking and action in safety improvement to be recognized, the final list of questions must be answered, not by safety professionals, but by business leaders. Safety strategy must be a business exercise, not a delegated activity to the safety professional or department.

Without strategy, is the achievement of new safety results more than luck? Is the inability to improve because of the intervention or other influences? Everyone wants excellence in safety performance and safety culture, yet we often forget excellence is not just about results; it is the confidence and ability to articulate why great results were achieved and knowing how to repeat and advance year after year.

Who Should Develop Corporate Safety Strategy?

For excellence in any operational category to be recognized, it is imperative employees make decisions and behave in alignment with the intended strategic direction. Safety is not a standalone strategy within a business; it must be an integral part of the overall operational plan. How clear is your strategic direction and how well can employees easily see the role safety plays within it?

Safety excellence is a strategic business decision and is fundamental to the overall direction, regardless of the purpose of the organization, profit or not-for-profit. Within high-performance organizations, the prioritization of energy, financial investment, the allocation of resources and the alignment of processes in safety is integral to the business strategy. This requires, for the sake of alignment, that business decisions be made by its leaders with counsel from safety experts, internally or externally. This presents the critical need for safety strategists within corporations.

The Delegation of Safety
You can't delegate a core value. Today, it is perceived as politically incorrect for an executive to say anything other than, "Zero incidents is our goal and safety is our top priority and core value." While of initial value, this thinking is limited. Like other important business functions, the specifics on how to accomplish these initial safety goals tend to be delegated to the subject matter expert. Again, if safety is indeed a core value, it cannot be delegated.

When an organization determines the need to place new emphasis on honesty, improving customer service, or improving trust within the company, this becomes a part of everyone's responsibility and a centerpiece to the overall strategy, the framework within which decisions and efforts are prioritized to accomplish goals and objectives. If these objectives are to be managed solely by a group, accomplished through a training program or delegated to a department, they eventually fail to gain the traction needed for a sustainable impact. Safety must be an integral piece of corporate strategy, and requires its own three- to five-year plan.

Developing the Three- to Five-Year Plan

Creating a vision of the future, understanding the current state, outlining a plan to improve or align with the vision, and measuring progress along the way are all fundamental parts of strategy in all businesses. Consider these core areas:

- Vision of the Future - Organizations focused on operational excellence realize the difference in excellence and success. Success that isn't repeatable, or to some degree predictable, isn't excellent. In safety, you cannot define excellence exclusively by lagging indicators, which tend to confirm trends but do not predict them. You must be focused, not just on the results, but also on what would be observable in the culture and performance that validates how the results were achieved.

- Strategic Priorities and Possibilities - What are the two or three areas that should be prioritized to make the vision a reality? What is the most important aspect to focus on to produce the greatest amount of prevention to risk exposure? What two or three focus areas would provide the most significant improvement in occupational culture? Most successful clients tend to rely on a comprehensive data-driven prioritization process that focuses on the dual areas of injury/incident prevention and cultural improvement.

Determining this, buttressed by data-driven decisions, allows for greater confidence in the prioritized goals and objectives that support the strategic priorities.

- Understanding the Current State - Assessing the current culture and systems without a strategy or destination in mind is to perpetuate program-of-the-month experiences, and effort-for-the-sake-of-effort thinking. The current-state assessment should provide an understanding of what will support or hinder the accomplishment of strategic priorities and prioritize based on value-add.

- Measurements of Progress - More organizations are taking the plunge to develop leading indicators and most are still focusing on the measurement of activities (e.g., number of near-misses reported, housekeeping audits, and behavioral observations) rather than indicators of how the activities are helping performance and progress toward the vision (e.g., increase in competence, knowledge, experience, proactive reliability, desired beliefs and behaviors). This would validate the course of action and the results, as well as help in predicting future performance.

<u>Key Strategic Questions</u>
To develop your comprehensive strategic framework that creates confident decisions in the prioritization of efforts to improve safety culture and performance, consider the following five questions when outlining your improvement objectives.

1. What are we trying to accomplish and why?
2. How will success and excellence be defined?
3. How well are our systems, resources, capabilities, focus and culture aligned with the strategic vision?

4. What data-driven process will help both proactively and reactively prioritize our injury/incident and cultural enhancement initiatives?
5. If we accomplish our objectives and meet our goals, what measurements indicate why and how it was achieved?

Who Establishes The Strategy?

Strategic planning and the development of a three- to five-year business plan is commonplace among corporate executives. Yet there appears to be a vacuum of methodology available to develop strategically-thinking safety leaders in most universities and corporations. Effective businesses already have effective strategic planning processes; let's not duplicate our efforts. Aligning safety and business strategy need not be a complicated process, unless, of course, we continue thinking tactically about how we prioritize safety efforts.

Competitive advantage in the marketplace no longer lies with managing and beating competition. Rather, it lies with creating and capturing new value with the customer, resulting in secured loyalty. Too often, attempts to improve safety include language such as "safety first," "safe production," and "safety mindset." The focus is on making safety a priority, a value, an integral responsibility. The perception, real or not, is that safety must compete with production. This is outdated thinking.

Safety Culture and Social Media

Social media will shape culture and improvement efforts at an increasing rate.

American culture has already been heavily impacted by social media. Cultures once formed around the workplace, school, church, or other places where people gathered to build relationships. Today, people can get together and form cultures in cyberspace. It is just a matter of time until these cyber cultures are tapped as a resource to build organizational and safety cultures.

Organizations that have been challenged by their own logistics now have a way to connect previously disconnected workers and to form safety cultures via social media. Already, Facebook and LinkedIn have invited companies to form their own groups online. Many companies have utilized the internet to distribute safety manuals and guidelines to their scattered workforces via shared, restricted-access websites. Adding opportunities for their workers to chat with each other and share ideas, experiences and better practices is a logical extension of internet and cell phone usage.

Although logistically-challenged organizations will be among the first to use social media, other organizations without logistical problems will follow in close order. We often joke about people sitting across a table texting each other rather than speaking. However, the joke is becoming the new reality. We are becoming more and more users of social media and texting, and less and less users of interpersonal conversation. Recognizing this reality is the first step toward forming company and safety cultures via social media.

Sharing everyday experiences and ideas in real time is a great lure to participation for workers. The ability to communicate accident-investigation findings immediately or even to have a safety stand down via everyone's smart phones could prove invaluable. Immediate access to another employee with greater expertise without travel could improve JSAs and other forms of pre-job planning.

The fact is workers already communicate with some of their fellow workers via social media. Groups of friends, family members at work, and neighbors who are also work associates often have friended each other and communicate regularly.

An organization can easily create a work community online to facilitate the connection of these groups. Several types of social media already facilitate multiple groupings of contacts such as family and friends. Adding business associates is a simple next step, for which the technology already exists.

Organizations are already experimenting with the utilization of social media to enhance safety in their cultures. The ones that were quickly successful had three commonalities in their approaches:

- First, they started with a beta group to prove the concept before expanding it to broader groups or organization-wide. The small groups were selected to be representative of organizational sub-cultures that already existed and had some degree of commonality and communication already. The problems encountered in each group were solved before expanding the cyber community to more members. Complex organizations selected more than one beta group, if they felt they were needed, to be a cross-section sampling of the overall organization.
- Second, the group member's experiences were monitored through surveys and focus group interviews to test the progress and analyze challenges. Overall usage of the media was also tracked to see what percent of participants used the media, how often and for how long. Length of comments and strings of dialogue were also measured to see if they were growing.
- Third, successful organizations made sure everyone had the same access to social media by providing the same types of smart phones to everyone in the groups and making sure everyone had adequate access and

instructions for using the site. Help desks were commonly provided for the users of the beta site through internal IT departments and help features were available through the social media programs used.

The organizations with successful beta groups began to expand the site offerings to larger groups in their organization. They were pleased with the beta groups and reported several perceived advantages which social media provided. The most common were:

- Interpersonal communication among workers increased drastically and barriers to talking to each other about safety issues seemed to disappear. Perceptions of the importance and contribution of fellow workers grew in relation to increased knowledge of what others were thinking and how they reacted to organizational issues. Perceptions of teamwork and looking out for each other in safety reached new heights.
- Communication of safety data improved. Accident and near-miss reports reached everyone via posts and were discussed among workers on the same social media. The testing of knowledge about recent events indicated much greater awareness of details and significance. Lessons learned from incidents were more widely known among workers. Communication of safety data was greatly enhanced and workers preferred getting the communication by social media rather than by more traditional communication methods.
- Perceptions of organizational leaders responding to safety suggestions changed radically. Workers felt leaders were more in touch with workplace issues and were listening to workers more openly. The need for formal suggestions was replaced by an ongoing dialogue between workers and leaders.

- Organizations with logistical challenges felt they were finally giving workers opportunities to network with each other and share best practices. The yearly meetings of limited numbers gave way to larger groups being able to get together daily.

These ideas only scratch the surface of what social media could potentially do for safety culture. Use and experience will teach the rest over time. Technology will be changing as fast as our ability to use it and that will open even more opportunities. Security of data will certainly be an issue, as it is already with all internet and broadcast media, but we will certainly run a race with hackers and cyber-crooks to stay ahead of their thievery.

Society, in general, is becoming a social media society. Savvy safety professionals will be getting together with their internal or outsourced information technology professionals, and with the growing group of cooperative providers to look ahead and explore the opportunities to utilize this world-changing social media to their advantage.

Key Points:

- Academic, single-science programs and processes, and the consultants who design and sell them, will be seen more as tools in the safety toolbox and less as silver-bullet or magic-pill solutions to safety.

- Safety will be considered another aspect of business management and company culture, rather than as utilizing science to manipulate worker behavior.

- Safety strategies will be developed, against which all programs will be judged and either continued, modified, or eliminated.

- Strategy and its methodology will incorporate more effective leading indicators providing timely insight that can be acted upon quickly and proactively.

- Safety and business strategy will be aligned and correlated to synergize rather than compete for resources and priority.

- The "more is better" mentality will give way to a focus on the quality and effectiveness of safety efforts.

- Safety goals will become more realistic and less idealistic, focusing on value-add rather than exclusively on injury and incident data. Goals will be motivational and achievable while not building a tolerance for any amount of failure.

- Social media will become a prominent force in shaping safety cultures as companies unite associates and give them networking opportunities online. This effort will undergo an awkward learning curve for both the media providers and organizations utilizing the media, but will ultimately revolutionize the speed and effectiveness of safety culture improvement.

Prediction #3: Leaders Actually Lead Safety

Roles of safety leadership will be redefined. Operational leaders will take a more hands-on role in safety, supported by an increase in clarity of responsibility and behavioral accountability. Safety will continue to become a line function with safety professionals taking a less hands-on and a more subject-matter expert and advisory role. Line management and supervisors will take a lead in workplace safety which will reduce the dichotomy between productivity and safety in the minds of workers. Supervisors and managers will train to be effective safety coaches rather than safety cops, and workers will be encouraged to continuously improve safety focusing on specific improvement targets.

When Leaders Don't Lead, Followers Won't Follow

At a recent dinner, I had an insightful conversation. I was performing a safety culture assessment of an organization in the oil & gas business. While at a restaurant, a man at the next table asked me who I worked for, as we were dressed alike. (I was wearing flame-resistant clothing due to the hazardous locations of the field interviews.)

Me: "ProAct Safety and you?"

Him: Not immediately answering but offering, "Safety's a bunch of BS."

Me: "I'm...sorry to hear that. What line of work are you in?"

Him: "I'm a Superintendent for..." (A known oilfield company. Also, a Superintendent is often the top local boss on construction and many oilfield projects.)

Me: "Oh yeah? Okay. So how did y'all do in safety last year?"

Him: "Well our rate was …" (It was quite poor).

Me: "That's quite unfortunate. Why do you think that is?"

Him: "Who knows? Probably if our leadership had a better attitude towards it."

Me: "So you are a Superintendent?"

Him: "Yeah."

Me, with an unfiltered response: "If you believe safety is a bunch of BS, what message do you think that sends to the guys you lead?" His facial expression was the only response I received.

Leaders must remember what they believe will influence their decisions and eventually be observable in their behaviors. If the leaders don't lead with the desirable beliefs and behaviors, don't expect the followers to follow. His unfortunate attitude (and possibly those of other leaders, if he was correct) might not be the only contribution to their poor performance, but it is certainly a good place to start.

<u>Who Really Owns Safety?</u>
If safety is more important than production, why does safety report up through Legal, Human Resources, or Production rather than production reporting up through the company's number one priority? If safety is so important, how many CEOs came from the safety department? Safety is a core value and most organizations employ safety managers. But if trust and honesty are also common corporate values, where are the

trust and honesty managers? The answer lies with the uncomfortable truth: reality.

Not intending to sound flippant, and recognizing the importance of process, passion, and the technical and legal reasons for safety professionals, I think asking who "owns" safety is an important issue to be analyzed if excellence is the goal.

Delegating responsibilities to individuals to drive improvement is logical and arguably necessary for any corporate executive. However, for safety to truly become infused into company decisions and behaviors, it cannot be delegated or managed by a corporate entity. When companies delegate responsibility to subject professionals to drive improvement, without a balance and measurement of contributed value, risks are encountered due to the obvious need to prove value and ensure employment stability.

In *Are CEOs Getting the Best From Corporate Function?*, Campbell, Kunisch and Muller-Stewens write, "Without sufficient guidance, corporate functions can become - often unintentional - self-serving. Instead of developing policies and processes to give divisions the practical support they want and need, corporate functions measure themselves against industrywide best practices or implement initiatives that increase their influence or simplify their own work. The result is often a lack of cooperation from operating managers."

While a bit of harsh commentary on outsourced function, there is an often observed truth. Safety professionals tend to measure themselves against the practices of what is perceived as great by other safety leaders, programs, methodologies or cultures, rather than what is great or perceived as excellent by the individual company they support. What is "best in industry" in safety will be different for each company, based on the practicality of how needs fit the reality of operations, budget constraint and corporate strategy. This should be determined by business, with advice from the safety professional, not the other way around.

Safety improvement is business improvement. As with any area of desired operational excellence, safety is only an aspect of your culture. It is not a stand-alone concept. While it is normal to tease out these aspects to better understand, manage, and improve them, we must realize when we focus on one part (safety culture), we often miss the forest for the trees (the role safety plays in, and is affected by, corporate culture). A company's entire culture, more than the aggregate safety beliefs and behaviors, influences the decisions and other operational priorities, perceptions and behaviors.

Consider a frequently-requested topic, such as providing safety leadership skills (e.g., performance feedback, coaching, counseling, accountability, communication, change-agent capabilities) to supervisory personnel. Is this safety leadership opportunity only benefiting safety, or all aspects of business? How much more support would be obtained if skills like these were viewed to be universally beneficial, rather than how to help one piece of operational performance advance?

In a recent article on why culture change efforts fail more often than not, Fred Kofman writes about his lessons learned attempting to change a culture, sponsored by the wrong individuals, aligned with the wrong goals and focused on activities rather than measurable business results. Most importantly was Kofman's lesson in sponsorship by a group (the corporate university) tasked with culture improvement, rather than the business leaders. "This created the perception that the CEO ran the business, while the corporate university ran the culture." He elaborates, "People felt pushed to attend activities that they saw as not part of their jobs. Culture became an additional thing to do, as opposed to the way to do everything."

Safety culture change, or any improvement in safety leadership (i.e., operational leader's safety roles, responsibilities and expected results), that is led by the safety department potentially sends the message that safety owns the safety aspect of the culture and the business leaders own the business. Doesn't this further silo, rather than integrate, safety responsibility?

It's a wonderful statement and a bit of a cliché to say that "Safety is everyone's responsibility." It has lost its meaning because most organizations have not effectively outlined the aforementioned safety leadership and hourly employee roles, and are rarely held accountable for expected behavioral performance in a timely and consistent fashion to make a substantial difference. Ultimately, the senior executives are responsible for both culture and performance in all facets of the business. This too, is reality.

Consultants Katzenbach and Aguirre, in an article on the CEO's responsibilities write, "If you are the chief executive of a company that is sailing with the wind and leading in its competitive race, that's a sign that your culture is in sync with your strategy. This makes your company much more likely to deliver consistent and attractive profitability and growth results. However, if your company is heading into stormy waters, facing the kinds of disruptive competition or unexpected market changes that affect every industry sooner or later, then a program of normal reinforcing leadership won't cut it. A culture that no longer aligns with your strategic and performance priorities needs a lot more attention - from you and other senior leaders."

Safety improvement is ultimately the responsibility of executive leadership. The cost of safety (e.g., injuries, insurance rates, damaged public image, production down-time, morale, employee disengagement) erodes shareholder value, and the value of safety (reliability, increase in quality, employee satisfaction, attractive employer) creates customer value. This discussion should not be new to the senior leader, as it's reminiscent of the modern quality movement. Consider your organization: forget platitudes, vision statements, and the desired reality. Who really leads safety? The business leaders or safety professionals? The answer will both define why you are achieving your current results and provide insight into the ability to achieve break-through performance.

Should the Safety Department Manage Safety?

The typical corporate organizational chart isn't what it used to be! It has gone from fat to flat, dotted lines have largely disappeared, and the safety department has been moved around like a chess piece. However, in many organizations, the safety professionals still fill a subject-matter-specific management role in safety. In such organizations, operational managers and supervisors tend to let the safety professionals manage safety while they take care of "business."

There are several potential problems with this model that have driven many high-performing organizations to make changes. The most common of these problems are as follows:

- It creates an artificial dichotomy between productivity and safety. Workers tend to get their priorities from their immediate supervisor. When the supervisor stresses getting the job done and someone else shows up with another set of priorities, like safety, the two tend to conflict. Workers begin to view safety as something that competes with their job. Safety doesn't become the way to work, but a distraction from work. Do they do the job or focus on safety? When pay increases and promotions come from production rather than safety, the dichotomy deepens even more.

- It lets production managers and supervisors "off the hook" for safety. If the safety person is in charge of safety, why should the production people worry about it? They feel free to concentrate on getting the product out the door or the services delivered. They can train people in job skills and let safety train them how to not get hurt. It drives the dichotomous thinking and excuses production from one of their key areas of responsibility. It also tends to separate the definitions of production and safety rather than establishing the more unified concept of safe production. Safety and quality should be an integral part of production and separating them creates an artificial and dangerous mentality that results in defects and accidental injuries.

- It distracts safety personnel from important support functions. When safety professionals have to be visible on the shop floor and make their presence felt, they develop a mentality of herding cats. They are chasing the risk-takers like desperate traffic cops rather than helping supervisors to become effective safety coaches. They don't have time to analyze data or develop proactive strategies when they are enforcers. If they are the ones who catch violators of safety policies, they are often the ones to handle the documentation and potential discipline through HR. They are already loaded with regulatory paperwork and trying to handle safety strategy as well as daily supervision and disciplinary issues, which usually means something gets neglected. It is human nature to take care of the urgent issues and neglect the important but less urgent ones.

- It stresses control over culture. The idea that workers must be "overseen" is counterintuitive to developing an effective safety culture. It takes more work up front to develop an excellent safety culture, but the effort is rewarded by decreased need for oversight and increased sustainability over time. Micromanagement is extremely counterproductive to cultural development. If safety professionals are constantly policing and managing the workers, they don't have time to improve the culture, and the very activity stealing their time is also working against the kind of culture they need to develop.

Changing the organizational chart alone is not the answer. The most common solution is to restructure the roles, responsibilities and results expected from both safety personnel and production managers and supervisors. This redefinition of job responsibilities may require some adjustment as well as additional training, but it has the potential to solve these common problems and to enable the safety culture to make a significant improvement.

Production takes on the day-to-day responsibilities of safety oversight with the workforce. Since they are already overseeing workers in other aspects of their jobs, the magnitude of this additional responsibility is not as great as usually anticipated. The definition of production is expanded to safe production. Safety is the way you do your job, not another set of standards or activities. The expectations change from units out the door to safe units out the door. Production managers communicate safety and lead by example. Safety is another topic of production rather than a competing priority. Production leaders lead safety training with the help of safety professionals. The dichotomy between production and safety begins to blur and then disappear.

Safety personnel become the subject matter experts (SMEs) and advisors to production managers and supervisors. They teach production people how to become safety coaches. The coaching models used are not specific to safety, but are rather performance coaching models that fit both productivity and safety issues. Supervisors become better developers of worker skills in all areas. Safety professionals now have time to proactively analyze safety data and suggest areas of focus that will have the greatest impact. These focus areas are reinforced by the supervisors through their safety coaching in the field. Safety personnel can now participate in safety training and meetings and sit on safety committees and executive safety councils. They can help to develop safety strategy and address the issues that help to form a strong safety culture.

Workers now view safety as an integral part of their job and a critical element of productivity. They intervene with fellow workers when supervisors are not there to do so. They have a strong internalized definition of safety and receive regular feedback on their performance. They are empowered rather than micromanaged. All their priorities come from the same source and there is no artificial division of safety and productivity. They are the same thing.

This model is not specific to any one industry or type of organization. It has been used in a wide variety of organizations from public to private sectors in everything from high-tech to no-tech industries. In many cases, the only things these organizations have in common is a desire for excellence in safety and a recognition that having the Safety Department manage safety is not the way to achieve it.

Five Vital Questions to Effectively Develop Leaders

Employee morale and behavior, results and culture are all the responsibility of organizational leadership. After all, if the leaders aren't leading, we can't expect the followers to follow, or be motivated to do so. In your organization, is leadership development thought of as best solved with a workshop or training event, or treated and funded as a business-critical, strategic priority?

Successful organizations realize everything rises and falls under leadership responsibility. These same organizations realize leadership development is not an event; it is an evolving process complementing all facets of business operations. Finally, they have key indicator measurements that provide insight and directs their continuous leadership investment.

"Teaching Supervisors to be Safety Coaches" and "Leadership Safety Coaching" have both played a significant role in developing leader capabilities (from lead employees to senior executives) in client organizations for twenty years. The successful organizations mentioned above represent how client organizations have followed a methodical process to prioritize their leadership improvement efforts because they realize failed leadership development approaches almost always create barriers to future attempts.

Whether you are developing leaders to improve safety, quality, productivity, or discretionary effort, the process is the same. Begin with answering the following five questions:

1. If we profiled a great leader in our operations, what would we see them doing and saying, and what results would we experience? Too many organizations seek to develop leaders without beginning first to identify and profile what a great leader would look like behaviorally. As the late Stephen Covey suggested, "Begin with the end in

mind." If you had excellent business results in all aspects of operations and a high-performing culture that sustains the results without stimulation, what would the average leader (level by level) be seen doing and saying that creates confidence?

2. What percent of leaders (level by level) would be placed in the category of change agents vs. managers of status quo and, more importantly, to whom does each leader report? Do you have the right people in the right positions with the right competencies and deploying the right leadership styles called for? Do you have more change agents or accepters of status-quo? This includes reporting structure. If a new supervisor is eager to demonstrate her desire to be an effective change-agent, yet reports up to a manager that is satisfied with status-quo, how long will this positive change attitude (or individual) last? This is why it is critical to not separate out a single level of leadership for development opportunities. People pay attention to what their boss pays attention to. If one level (i.e., supervisor) doesn't see the new leadership style or skills demonstrated by the level above, all improvement opportunity may be lost.

3. What do we want the intended audience to feel, know, and do as a result of this initiative, and how will we validate the impact? Emotions have an impact on behavioral choice and humans respond emotionally to new information before they respond logically. Is there an intended emotion that is being solicited? For knowledge, several organizations conduct pre- and post-tests to validate both the existing and transference of new knowledge. But there is more to leadership development than knowledge alone and it can be

results-limiting to stop there. For example, if leaders already know what you want them to know, but the gap is in behavior, then more knowledge isn't the answer. This is why all leadership development efforts must have a behavioral focus. If targeting safety leadership, what are the behavioral objectives? Are the desired behaviors of leaders to be focused on the prevention of injuries and incidents and strengthening the safety culture? Finally, what measurement systems will support your ability to measure what people feel, know, and do as a result of your training? This will be critical to demonstrate both return on investment and return on attention.

4. How will this effort contribute to business results? If leadership development solicits the desired emotional response, knowledge increases, and positive observable behavior increase, but the results do not change, it is common for support to wane and for barriers to future effort to be created. Results must be more than just lagging indicators. What increase in activities and performance would be experienced when the efforts are successful?

5. What systems, methodologies, and experiences would complement or hinder this effort? All leadership development efforts are only as effective as the reinforcement that follows. Current performance management (i.e., only annual reviews), measurements, systems, culture, and hiring and promotion processes are just a few influencers on leadership styles. Answering this question is a must to prevent surprises down the road. Most leadership development methodologies do not fail in theory, they fail in practice when not well thought out in advance of the first exercises.

Most effective executives, when discovering the need to improve leadership capabilities within their organization, demand a quick response because of the realized substantial potential in the investment. There can be a remarkable difference in doing things right versus right now. Rather than starting by seeking out the best program, workshop or training material, ensure there is alignment in the vision of excellence and the starting point of your leaders. Sometimes it's necessary to take a step back in order to leap forward.

For Sustainable Safety, Leaders Must Do More Coaching, Less Policing

<u>Pushing workers to only obey the rules and wear PPE typically creates minimal effort safety cultures without proactive employees.</u>

Is your goal to exercise control over your employees or to create a motivated workforce inspired to go above and beyond and continuously ask of each other, "Are we currently the best we can be?"

"Flow," proposed by Mihaly Csikszentmihalyi, a leading researcher on positive psychology, is a state of being in which a person is fully focused and involved in the successful outcome of a task. Flow is the best working definition of desirable, intrinsic motivation. This means there is no incentivizing, forcing, threatening or competitive environment to create an outcome. The desire to achieve is purely internal.

To create sustainable, above-and-beyond performance in others, you must create a situation in which an individual feels motivated to provide the critical discretionary effort. Preaching the necessity of certain behaviors and the penalty for non-conformance does more harm than good. Motivating someone to do something typically results in either short-term behavioral change or the creation of behaviors to avoid further "motivation."

Charlie 2-2-3

Let's look at the example of Michael. Early in Michael's career, he was a safety compliance officer for an oilfield company. His role was to inspect company-owned locations for compliance with government and company standards. Unfortunately, the fact that he was a caring individual with a passion for the safety and well-being of others mattered little. He was known as a "safety cop".

Michael told me the following story of when he realized he was perceived in this manner. It hit during his third visit on a company location to audit and provide feedback. On his visits, Michael would arrive, exit his company vehicle, put on his personal protective equipment (PPE) and walk toward the entrance. Just before he was to enter the facility, he would hear over the loudspeaker, "Charlie 2-2-3, Charlie 2-2-3."

On his third visit, he realized "Charlie 2-2-3" was code for "The safety guy is on site." This prompted people to begin using their horns while operating forklifts and to properly wear their PPE. This is when Michael realized he was indeed a "safety cop".

I hold first-responders in the highest regard. Yet, the sad reality is, while police officers work aggressively to create positive images of themselves, they are often perceived as those who issue tickets and fault-find rather than as the problem-solvers and problem preventers that they are. This holds true for people with safety responsibility; they are seen as problem creators rather than as operational excellence advisers.

It's Not One Person's Responsibility

More organizations are relying less on having safety personnel on location on a daily basis to ensure compliance because they are concerned that safety will be viewed as one person's responsibility, rather than everyone's responsibility. More and more, organizations are creating ownership in and responsibilities for safety at multiple levels, including those in a management, supervisory or team leader positions, rather than relying solely on a safety professional to own it all and do it all

At conferences, I am very fortunate to speak alongside many senior executives of companies who truly understand the role safety plays among the hyper-competitiveness of organizational priorities. It is often said by these individuals, "Good safety is good business."

Many organizations that use contractor services are measuring delivery capabilities by more than the standard performance indicators. These customers are increasingly concerned about their contractors' safety performance and are developing the perspective, as shared to me privately by one executive recently, "If you can't manage something as important as safety, well, what else are you not able to do well?"

If an organization can accomplish incredible performance outcomes at the sacrifice of employee safety, what does this say about the long-term viability of the company? Moreover, if safety can be sacrificed and profit is the sole driving force, it is not long until negative performance indicators are realized in quality, customer service, delivery and competency.

Inspire, Don't Manage
Managing for compliance is a fundamental aspect of any successful safety management system, but what is "management"? The average definitions for management range anywhere from control, handling, or direction over

behavior, to aligning groups or individuals to accomplish goals in the best manner possible.

The foundation for safety excellence has two parts: management and influence. Management is critical to help a group become compliant and ensure groups act in alignment for recognition of performance targets. Influencing grows in importance when we recognize the limitations of compliance on the path toward sustainable excellence.

American businessman Lee Iacocca once said, "Any supervisor worth his salt would rather deal with people who attempt too much than those who try too little." We need to create cultures where people feel safe to innovate. Working only to obey the rules, follow the procedures and wear PPE ensures no one experiences a compliance-related injury. It also typically creates a culture that works hard to ensure that minimal effort becomes common practice, and does little to guarantee people are proactive in their personal risk identification and mitigation/removal efforts.

This desirable state can be recognized only when people feel motivated and trust the systems in which their performance is measured and in the people who measure it. If you want new results, people have to be inspired, not managed.

Proven Coaching Model
When I ask audiences to think of a person who has provided great inspiration and successfully motivated a team or group of people, the predominant answer is a coach. The purpose of a coach is to help others work toward their strengths and be the best they can be. A coach is not a problem-performance manager; this more often falls into the category of counseling.

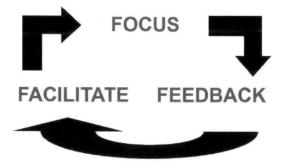

Focus, feedback and facilitation make up this three-part coaching model for safety. Focus addresses what you want the individual to do; feedback entails positive reinforcement and the expression of concern; and facilitation means removing roadblocks from employees' paths to successful behavior.

The following three-part coaching model has been extremely successful:

- **Focus** - What specifically do you want the individual to do? Certainly it is encouraged to allow people to maintain a sense of autonomy in much of what they do. In safety, if there are behaviors or precautions known to minimize or eliminate risk exposure, this often becomes an organizationally aligned coaching focus. Rather than solely concentrating communication around desirable results, which is more typical than we admit, can you behaviorally describe what actions are necessary to accomplish a desirable target? If yes, can your employees? If they cannot, the focus is not aligned.

- **Feedback** - The most effective forms of feedback for performance coaching are positive reinforcement (designed to encourage specific behavior to continue) and the expression of concern (designed to help break complacency, raise awareness, understand risk-taking in a non-confrontational manner, and talk through alternatives).

- **Facilitate** - Make it easy for employees to successfully accomplish the tasks in the safest and most successful manner possible. Providing focus and feedback is valuable when there are no obstacles or barriers in their way. Sometimes a leader has to create the path for someone to be successful. This requires the removal of roadblocks to ensure the desirable behavior is possible.

Moving Forward

Helping supervisors to become safety coaches has provided significant value for hundreds of organizations, even outside of safety. The skills provided to coach for safety performance can easily be leveraged to coach for other areas of operational performance.

American author, Mark Victor Hansen, said, "In imagination, there's no limitation." Cops are perceived to penalize people. Coaches help individuals achieve what they previously believed was impossible. This is the role of a great leader. What role will you play today?

Key Points:

- Leadership of safety will migrate back to organizational leaders and not be delegated to safety professionals. Safety professionals will direct or assist with the implementation of the safety strategy developed by the organizational leaders.

- Supervisors will be trained and held accountable to be safety coaches within their work teams.

- Safety professionals will begin to transform from managers to organizational resources and subject-matter-expert.

- This will all result in greater employee engagement and a continuous-improvement mindset.

Prediction #4: Grunt to Guardian to Guru

The role of the company safety professional, which has already begun to evolve from busy work to management, will be more clearly defined and focused on contributing value through subject-matter expertise. Day-to-day workplace oversight of safety will no longer be the primary responsibility of the safety professional.

Safety strategy: Is your safety professional a grunt or guru?

Safety professionals play many roles (e.g., trainer, enforcer, coach, adviser, facilitator, and consultant). We have all had days where we oscillated between them all. Eventually, to advance the safety capabilities and maturity of the organizations they support, safety professionals must move on from being a doer, enabling others to take on the responsibilities. The safety professional then becomes an adviser, setting the vision and influencing progress toward it.

Advisers are more than technical experts; rather, they are individuals able to see the bigger picture and help others see the value in making the right decisions in support of the needed direction. This requires advisers to not only have a firm grasp on safety improvement possibilities, but also the business reality they will be implemented within.

As pointed out in our first book together, *STEPS to Safety Culture Excellence*, safety culture is a part of organizational culture and should not be managed independently. The business tools that serve industry so well to dominate market share can and should be used to dominate the attention share, a measurement of cultural focus. Strategically thinking safety

56

professionals recognize the need to move from grunt, to guardian, to guru within their own organizations.

A grunt is a person performing the specific tasks for others (i.e., lead this safety meeting). Guardians oversee the grunts and others (e.g., supervisors, operations managers, contractors) who perform the efforts that were previously owned and carried out solely by the grunts. The gurus become the subject matter experts, offering counsel to shape the business and individual decisions that drive the performance and culture within organizations. Becoming a guru necessitates moving the thinking from tactical to strategic, and formulating a safety business plan in collaboration with business leaders to ensure fit and practicality.

Since the first use of strategy within business operations in the 1960s, organizational leaders have worked diligently to identify and continuously improve their strategic planning process, ensuring the proactive prioritization of focus and resources that result in the ability to accomplish forecasting confidently. However, as Helmuth von Moltke, a 19th century Prussian Army leader, wisely observed, "No battle plan ever survives first contact with the enemy." Successful organizations develop key performance indicators to monitor the progress of the executed strategy to ensure progress toward the intended direction.

Unlike activity-based measurements, performance measurements help an organization not only see if they are staying the course, but also provide the insight that zero-based indicators miss when used alone. When great results are attained, confidence should encompass the safety leader when providing what the forecasting business leaders require of the three- to five-year strategic safety plan.

Without a clear vision for safety excellence, data-driven and proactively prioritized objectives, and measurements of both progress and results, organizations will remain with grunt-like safety professionals, diligently overseeing the implementation of program after program. Certainly, there is value for these types of individuals. However, if safety improvement means searching for the next program, this demonstrates tactical thinking and will hinder the ability to evolve past being "good" in safety. Fundamentally, it comes down to answering the important, yet telling, question, "Do we want to be excellent in safety or get a little better next year?" This will determine the level of thinking needed in your safety professional.

The Ideal Safety Career Path

Safety professionals are so busy they don't always think about their own future. Those who do often describe a desire to move from the position of site safety manager to a regional, and then a corporate level. When we ask them how they plan to do so, the usual response is, "By doing a really good job!"

We would like to suggest that safety professionals plan their own career path strategically and follow their plan meticulously. This plan will work both for those moving up the corporate ladder and for those happy to stay where they are but maximize their current position. It will increase effectiveness and efficiency, as well as job satisfaction.

Whether trying to plan a career that climbs the corporate ladder or expands a current position, plan how to expand your value to the organization. One can do this in stages and each stage will make them more valuable whether moving up or staying put. Here are the three stages through which a safety professional should move in the course of a successful career:

Stage 1: Grunt – Almost every career begins with grunt work. Paperwork, daily routine, busywork and common tasks dominate time and challenge endurance. This work isn't given to beginners because it is easy; it's given because it is basic. It still requires skill, organization and an eye for detail to get it done in a timely and efficient manner. Individuals will become more accurate and more cognizant of the value of such work and the data produced. When this type of activity is mastered, one can look to the future. The true calling is not to stay busy, but to make a difference. Begin to automate, handoff or minimize the daily grunt work and start to take care of the workforce.

Stage 2: Guardian – In this stage, the professional begins to move beyond the daily chores to the oversight of safety. They begin to see the big picture and take care of issues before they get out of hand. They quit trying to do everything for everyone and just make sure it gets done. If help is available, the crucial skills of delegation and oversight are learned. They realize that safety is not so much what the safety professional does as much as what workers and leaders do. They help them do it instead of trying to do it themselves. The workers begin to view the safety professional as a resource rather than a workhorse, and their sphere of influence grows.

If the safety professional becomes an effective guardian, they will find themselves overseeing more efforts than they could possibly do alone. They help the whole organization effectively manage safety and serve as a guide and resource. These efforts are significantly more valuable to the organization than grunt work. The safety professional can now make more of a difference in safety than before. They can lead safety efforts and give them direction and meaning. Their example and expertise inspires the entire organization to pursue excellence in safety.

Stage 3: Guru – It takes a lot of climbing to see safety from thirty-thousand feet. That is why all the grunt work and guardianship pays off, because that is what helps them see the big picture clearly. At this level, they work on strategy rather than tactics or implementation. They help the organizational leaders to develop and deploy effective strategies for safety excellence. They are truly the expert who can map the path forward and solve the problems along the way. They have seen how other efforts got derailed or delayed and they build safeguards against such problems into their strategies. They warn others of potential pitfalls and help them avoid common problems. They become the critical thinker whose insight and point of view have stand-alone value to the organization.

The safety professional can now develop others into safety grunts and guardians, and help them along the progression to their own level. They are now the ultimate safety resource. They can work at any level and help others do so. They can help leaders more effectively lead safety and turn supervisors into effective safety coaches. They can paint the big picture to new employees and start them on careers that include excellent safety performance. When new approaches to safety come along, they can evaluate their effectiveness and potential fit into their organization's safety strategy.

At the guru level, they will need to continually feed on new ideas and methods. They will need to belong to safety organizations, attend conferences and read the latest safety publications. They will need to become a reader of books; not just safety books, but also business books. They will quit seeing safety as a separate part of the business and envision how it belongs to a unified whole. They will help leaders position safety as a part of producing goods and/or services rather than a conflicting priority. They will help leaders realize that managing safety is the ultimate indicator of how they manage the business.

The organization will reach a level of safety performance that will qualify it to do business with the very best in your industry. The safety professional's continued guidance and strategic development of safety processes and metrics will become an integral part of the overall excellence of the organization's performance. They and other organizational leaders will find synergies in their efforts and will borrow ideas to improve other aspects of business. They will take their place with the other organizational leaders and provide the highest level of value possible.

One can look at their career strategically and begin to take steps toward the next stage. They should get into the habit of continuous, lifetime learning. They should network with those in safety at the next level and make contacts with good mentors when they attend conferences or visit other sites. They should form a support network of like-minded individuals in their field who can also see and value these three stages of growth and development and begin their journey. When one climbs the ladder of personal worth, the corporate ladder will take care of itself.

Key Points:

- Safety professionals will continue to evolve in their roles from grunts (workers) to guardians (managers) to gurus (subject-matter experts and advisors).
- Career paths in many organizations will drive this progression.
- The education of safety professionals will evolve to support their new roles.
- Changing the job descriptions of safety professionals will greatly affect the job descriptions of first-line supervisors.

Prediction #5: A New Kind of Safety Consultant Will Emerge

Safety consultants who assist safety professionals will remain, but evolve. They will help the safety professional become the expert and to advise the organization. Some of these will continue to be academic experts on various human sciences and their consulting will be based on their expertise.

A whole new type of safety consultant will emerge who will interface with organizational leaders rather than safety professionals and will aid with strategy development and cultural alignment. These consultants will not be academics, but business professionals, and their consulting will be based not on their expertise, but on the organization's needs.

Consultants vs. Culture: Can the Two Work Against Each Other?

For the past three decades, two trends in safety have been on a collision course: the use of safety consultants and the inevitable focus on improving safety culture. Why a collision? Because any form of outsourcing is potentially hazardous to a culture, which is a sharing of internalized values and practices. Controlling the influences on culture is necessary for excellence and opening the door to outsiders can seriously compromise that control. However, this collision is avoidable if the potential for it is recognized and intelligently managed.

Organizational downsizing has been a significant influence on this issue in two different ways. First, downsizing has impacted culture. Lean organizations often lose opportunities for contact between employees, which can otherwise be culture building. Reducing the workforce inevitably eliminates key members of the culture and causes a re-defining of the group. It also often increases the pace of work and the diversity of tasks each remaining worker inherits.

Second, downsizing makes the use of outside expertise necessary, as specialists and subject-matter experts were eliminated from their internal positions. Organizations decide they can hire outside expertise when they need it more efficiently than they could keep highly paid experts on staff. While downsizing enabled some organizations to better focus on their core competencies, it also redefined their culture and the relationship to certain experts who can influence it.

The focus on safety culture is the natural maturing of safety efforts. We began with traditional controls over conditions and behaviors that impact safety. We made the workplace safer and then focused on the worker in that workplace. As we mastered the basics and overcame the highest-probability risks, we began to realize that we cannot control everything. Some aspects of safety are still impacted by individuals and groups and the dynamics they develop. Some precautions don't need to be rules or procedures, but need to be adopted as common practice by the people who do the work. Leaders can influence such group dynamics, but there are other influences as well. Few organizations reach true excellence in their safety performance without addressing these cultural influences.

Since many organizational leaders know little about safety, they seek expert help. Consultants have assisted with the workplace design and upkeep, with addressing worker behaviors, and now with safety culture. The use of outside expertise is not, in and of itself, the problem. It is the way in which such expertise is used that makes the crucial difference. Outside experts can actually help strengthen the culture if they are utilized correctly. Unfortunately, there are two reasons why this seldom happens.

The first reason lies within the consultants and their business model. Since managers seek expertise, consultants try to impress with their credentials and turn their expertise into a product for sale. This usually entails turning science into technology. The one expert cannot personally service enough clients so he or she develops a process based on expertise but dummied down so lesser consultants can deliver it. To maintain uniformity and quality control over many consultants, the process for sale must be basically the same for every client. This means it may not be a good fit for the culture. Many processes have a degree of flexibility to allow for a better fit, but there are still more unique cultures than unique consulting products and processes.

The second reason consultants are often misused to the detriment of culture is simply that managers tend to delegate tactics rather than develop strategy for safety. The lack of an overarching strategy for safety means that there is no standard by which to judge a consultant's product other than the sales pitch. Is this product a good fit with a strategic goal or just a tactic to move a number in the desired direction? Any time something as critical as safety is delegated to an outside source, you risk sending the message that 1.) Safety is not an integral part of the culture; 2.) Safety is separate from (and not as important as) other priorities that are not delegated to outsiders; and 3.) The organization does not really know how to make safety happen within its own management systems. Any or all of these messages are potential safety culture killers.

The proper utilization of outside expertise is not overly complicated, but it usually takes more work on the part of organizational leaders. Experts should be utilized as gurus, not as grunts. They should be strategic advisors at the highest level, not implementers at the lowest levels. This necessitates that leaders realize the need for a safety strategy and not just a program to lower accident rates. Other core values of the organization are not delegated or addressed without strategic thinking and planning, neither should safety. Experts can greatly assist in strategic thinking and the organization can gain a clear vision of where they want to go and how to get there. Experts can also help assess current status to better enable navigating toward desired goals.

Once the strategy is set and the vision is shared, it is critical that the steps of the journey be lead from within the organization. This does not mean that experts cannot be utilized to advise and assist at each level. It means that the strategy must be internalized and complete delegation makes internalization difficult or impossible. At some point the student must take over from the master. This means that the utilization of outside experts should have a well-planned disengagement, not a long-term dependency.

Just like any tool or resource, outside expertise can lead to help or harm. As we turn our attention to safety culture as the next potential step change toward excellence, it is crucially important that we understand the potential impact for good and evil that safety consultants can make. Make sure that any consulting project is based on the strategic needs of your culture and not just the expertise or product of the consultant.

Key Points:

- Traditional safety consulting will change significantly.
- Safety consultants will begin to fall into two categories:
  - Those who work directly with safety professionals to provide technical expertise and detailed compliance information for the safety efforts, and
  - Those who work more with leaders and supervisors to offer strategic help, personal coaching and training. This type of consulting will be based on the needs of the client, not the expertise of the consultant.

Prediction #6: Safety Programs Will Begin to Change Their Focus

The following will be the new focus of safety programs:

- The focus of safety programs will begin to change from control to marketing.
- Workers will begin to be viewed as the customer of safety efforts rather than a problem to be controlled.
- Safety training will seek buy-in, not merely knowledge transfer.
- Success in safety will be gauged by value added, not solely by accident reduction.
- Safety improvement efforts will become more fit-for-purpose with a focus on transference of value.

Safety Must Deliver More Than Customers Expect

The goal of marketing strategy is often to beat the competition. If safety sets a goal to beat the competition it has already failed. One of the major competitors of safety in most organizations is production. If safety succeeds in beating production, it kills the business. If it fails, it is often because it was defeated by production. This is why we must have a strategy that supports, rather than conflicts with, business strategy. Business strategy eats safety strategy all day long.

Real strategy is a framework of choices the organization makes to capture and deliver value. Strategy is: "How do we win?" Future safety improvement efforts will focus on corporate safety strategy. Far too many organizations do not have a true strategy for safety excellence.

Zero injuries, engagement, and hearts and minds are all by-products - not the goal or focus - when safety evolves to first capture and deliver value. Take a hard look. Do our communications, meetings, programs, evaluations, and observations add value? Do we create excitement? Do we have potential customers standing in line to be a part of what we all know is important and adding value on and off the job?

Successful companies must deliver new, even unanticipated, value or they lose market share to those that do. Safety can create this type of value - with a strategy and focus on delivering more than the customers know they need. If the perceived value of safety is only achieving zero injuries, why will you be needed once you provide that to your customers?

There will be an increasing amount of conversation and methodology available to organizations to help answer the important questions to determine what to do and not to do. Managing and leading safety is like all other aspects of business. Tradeoffs are made on a routine basis designed to capture and deliver value to the customer. When we start focusing on winning, we recognize that zero injuries is the byproduct of the value of safety excellence, not the main goal.

Finding Support: From Reducing Costs to Adding Value

Do you view safety as a cost center or a value contributor to the organization? What about your operational leadership? What should you do if you find yourself supporting those who do not support you and your efforts? The answer often lies in what people see value in, your role in it, and how you are selling the value of safety. Yes, you need to sell safety if you desire more than compliance behavior!

Increasingly, companies are realizing not just the altruistic aspect of safety but also the significant business costs of poor safety performance. Many of our clients will not do business with any vendor, regardless of their service offering, if they have poor safety performance.

While this support for safety results by executive leadership is admirable thinking for the safety professional, caution is advised. An exclusive focus on safety lagging indicator performance can drive the wrong behavior in many well-intended leaders. For example, if zero injuries is our only goal, let's punish those who report and we will achieve zero injuries! Obviously, this is not an ethical route. Results themselves are of value, but how they are achieved is often more important.

Great managers not only lead others to great performance, but have profound insight into how the results were achieved, safety or otherwise. This has led many new organizations to explore their safety excellence strategy and realize they don't really have one. How much value is lost here?

The value of fewer injuries, incidents, and regulatory issues is easy to affix a cost savings to. But when you start to see the value of safety excellence in contributions to the business strategy, new value opportunities emerge. Consider, if the safety strategy is purposeful, yet not so aggressive that it restricts business growth, everyone wins. If the safety strategy is too weak or reactive, hard and soft safety costs will follow the growth strategy as the safety professionals mop up after the financial decisions are executed.

Think of the unforeseen employee and regulatory costs that could have easily vetted out if safety leadership played a role in the diligence process. There are many ways to determine the value safety provides, but it takes an educational process, sharing of information, and understanding what others are doing and why they are doing it, to truly gain the right insight.

Leaders need to see the cost of safety excellence as a value-add to the organization (how it helps in productivity and client acquisition) and not view it as a cost center to manage. To facilitate this, focus on two aspects that will increase the perception of value of safety with most people, from leaders to temporary workers. 1.) Is it as efficient as it could be? Look at safety efforts: is it efficient or is there unnecessary waste? 2.) Does it capture and deliver value for its customers? If we aren't delivering value, we have cultures of have-to rather than want-to.

Ultimately we must realize that with all the best intent, you can't make people care and you can't force an epiphany. If some are not open to a new way of thinking, others will be. This is why we will only work with executives that demonstrate they truly care about the people, not just the numbers. Life is too short to spend your time frustrated with those who simply don't care. Find leaders who want to be efficient in safety and deliver the customers new exciting value, every day. Then, everyone wins.

Licensing and Royalty Fees Can Blunt Safety Advances

Practices to improve safety performance and culture have and will continue to evolve, due to advances in thinking born from a continuous pursuit to challenge the status quo. But who should own these advancements and what rights will exist to modify and improve upon them? When an organization is hindered in the ability to internally train and modify, or evolve methodology and programs, it creates an unhealthy dependency on external organizations, slows the rate of continuous improvement and ultimately creates a barrier to safety excellence.

The safety industry, along with the rest of the world, is quickly approaching a new industrial revolution, observed by the increase in do-it-yourself and internally-led projects, a significant rise in independent consultants and the mass and rapid spreading of new ideas. And it's all available with a simple search within your favorite web browser. Operational and safety improvement concepts previously resided in only those with the time to file a patent and the capital and resources to mass-produce. The world is changing, both in the ability to innovate and also in the way innovation must be utilized for the global advancement of safety.

Industrial Revolutions and the Impact on Innovation

Between 1750 and 1850, the world and basis of societies changed like never before, moving from a culture centered on manual labor and farming to machine-based manufacturing. Large-scale innovations (e.g., roads, mining, metal manufacturing) were created to support the changes in living arrangements and spending habits. This time period (The First Industrial Revolution) was appropriately dubbed the Capitalist Economy.

The Second Industrial Revolution (Technological Revolution) occurred between 1867 and 1914, resulting in the invention and exploitation of new technologies (e.g., electricity, internal combustion engines, chemicals) facilitating mass production. Still, to this point, much of innovation was largely controlled by growing corporations and supported through the creation of management and organizational sciences.

Over the past couple of decades, control of idea-ownership and even employment has moved from large to small employer, and even self-employed. Today in the U.S., the small businesses combined have become, by far, the largest employer.

In his new book, *Makers: The New Industrial Revolution*, bestselling author, Chris Anderson, calls the third revolution "the industrialization of the Maker Movement". While the book was primarily a sequel to his first book, *The Long Tail*, Anderson predicts the increase of a greater, amateur, do-it-yourself (DIY) movement, facilitated by an increase in capability of creative digital and personal manufacturing. He points out how much easier it has become to imagine and then produce something innovative. While the book is slanted more towards technological innovation, it is important to recognize the same themes are becoming more obvious in the safety industry.

Today, a reader can explore any major source of social media (e.g., Facebook, Twitter, LinkedIn) with the search term "safety" and new innovative ideas, products, methodologies and tactics are quickly discovered. This new idea-manufacturing capability is now facilitating organizations on the continuous journey to safety excellence, as they evolve past the "find and adopt a best-practice" thinking and recognize there is always a better way. These same companies seek outside ideas to prevent the not-invented-here occupational hazard Lisa Gansky calls "breathing your own exhaust".

The capabilities and control of idea manufacturing and proliferation has expanded beyond large conglomerates dominating the methodology marketplace to today's melting pot of potential approaches. For companies to progress and continuously improve, the internal capability must exist to make the methodology of change fit the company culture, logistical challenges and operational realities.

When ideas to improve safety are regulated by a pay-me-first requirement, profit is being put in front of safety, which slows the advancement of safety excellence cultures. I can appreciate trademarking terms, software or specific detailed methodologies for the protection and continuance of the business and individuals who create them. I, too, participate in such things. After all, without the revenues derived from such developments, businesses would not be able to afford the capital needed to test and discover such advancements. However, protecting new ideas behind offerings where learning can only occur after payment is received, is placing profit in front of safety.

The safety profession should encourage the advancements of ideas and idea ownership, but there needs to be a healthy balance on availability and flexibility of usage. Additionally, it is not as simple as moving from one polar end (It is mine!) to another (open source). Consider how iTunes has changed the way music is consumed. Not too long ago, an entire album was purchased for the benefit of a single song. Now, the customer can select this single song based on preference and value, which enables the artist to focus on individual value-add with each offering, rather than lumping non-value-add to fill an album revolving around a hit single.

Ideas to advance safety must progress similarly, based on value, and should not create dependency between vendor and client. Further, methodologies must be internalized to facilitate sustainability. Many organizations, and the safety industry included, have grown in size due to this dependency and have been funded by the umbilical cord of royalties or program-for-rent payments. From a business perspective, this makes sense, especially if shareholder value and profit growth are the underlying reasons, but there certainly must be a better way.

This complicated issue is not solved through a single writing, nor is this the intent of this piece. However, there are questions that have served well to determine value, flexibility and longevity of idea acceptance. Whether innovator or potential consumer, consider utilizing these questions as decision filters:

1. In practice, how will this further the journey to an incident-free workplace and Safety Culture Excellence?
2. Will this further the ability to internally improve and sustain results, or will it create dependency?
3. How flexible is this for internal usage regardless of culture and operational reality?
4. How effectively, yet quickly, can internalization occur?
5. How does this further the ability to execute the safety excellence strategy?
6. Does the acceptance of the idea provide more long-term value to creator or consumer?
7. Who is responsible and accountable for what?

Safety excellence isn't just about achieving great results; it is also about sustaining them. With the global recession of the past several years, organizations of all sizes regressed in their safety performance due to the inability to pay licensing or royalty fees. While creators and owners of ideas should be compensated based on value, we must further examine and agree on the reason for advancements in sciences, technology, programs and tools in safety. If the creators are mostly driven by profit, barriers to safety excellence will be experienced by their consumers. If, however, the creator and client collaborate to experience and focus on value and equitable compensation, justified by the furthering of safety performance and culture, everyone wins and the question of who owns the ability to advance safety becomes clear.

The Futility of RFPs

When your organization has a problem or opportunity, you put together a Request for Proposals (RFP) and send it to the individuals and/or firms you consider to be leaders on the subject. Then you pour over their responses like resumes, hoping to find a glimmer that separates one from the rest. Not finding any such differentiator, you go with the lowest price, sign a contract and begin the project. What is wrong with this picture?

Unfortunately, the answer is much larger than the scope of this article, but let me point out a few key issues:

Selection Criteria - Do you want the cheapest or the best? Do you want the best solution or the best proposal? When you select your provider based on a "writing project", you roll the dice. The large consulting firm may hire the best proposal writer and the weakest consultant. They may specialize in something completely foreign to your needs but can make a convincing argument. The lone practitioner who is worth his salt doesn't have time to complete your hundred-page questionnaire if he or she is currently doing projects for other clients. The best experts in any field have learned that they don't have to do your dog-and-pony show because their reputation and client referrals keep them busy without such efforts. So who do you attract with your RFP?

Scope Creep - I have had Presidents and CEOs of large organizations tell me that avoiding scope creep on projects was their primary goal for utilizing RFPs. That sounds logical if, in fact, you have accurately and completely identified and defined the scope of your project. Most RFPs either broadly define the issue or assume an off-the-shelf solution is best and want it bid like a commodity. You are asking the doctor to prescribe before diagnosing. You are giving the problem solver the solution and asking for a price. What if there is a better, more cost-effective solution than your RFP assumes? Since the consultant was not involved in assessing the problem or opportunity, they will discover the details as they go. That almost guarantees scope creep!

Everyone fears the auto mechanic telling you that your $59.95 brake job has just turned into a $600 project and $1,000 worth of new tires, but the opposite can be true as well. I was once asked to develop an organization-wide half-day training program to solve a problem. I solved the problem with $50 worth of printing of pocket cards that reminded maintenance people of an 11-step process they were often forgetting and doing in the wrong order. A large governmental organization sent me an RFP and I responded with a letter suggesting a better, more cost-effective solution that the RFP did not list. I got the project.

Internal Resource Requirements - Since most RFPs result in a contract that specifies time, deliverables and the associated costs, the provider is incentivized for using the maximum time to complete the job. That usually means that they will maximize the inconvenience to you and tie up your internal resources helping them do their project in a less-than-efficient way. Fees based on time spent are a norm in most RFPs and almost always result in waste. Since you have contracted to pay for the provider's time, you consider that a given, but what about their use of your internal resources? What is the opportunity cost of getting the job done in the maximum time allowed by the contract? What could your workers have accomplished in the extra time they spent on this project?

Relationship - Often, RFPs are used to select a firm. The actual person who delivers the services is unknown until the project is initiated. Personal relationships are sometimes as important as skills when working on organizational issues. The wrong person talking to the president or delivering the training to the maintenance department can undo the whole project. At best, if the person is a good fit, their relationship is now defined by hours and deliverables rather than results or long-term, value-added relationships. Certainly the provider will try to impress that they can add future value if their firm rewards them for such action, but will you get the same provider if you hire the firm again? Seldom does an RFP result in true "partnering" between leaders and subject-matter experts. Such partnering has produced results far beyond "project completed" thinking. And these ongoing relationships continue to add value as providers learn more about organizational needs and opportunities.

Results - Even though most RFPs were developed to get results, they get effort instead. When you pay for effort and have a narrowly defined scope, your own people hesitate to ask the provider to finish up or add another piece because they know it will result in extra costs and contract revisions. The RFP and resulting contract can actually keep your organization from getting the results you want. You want great results for the organization and reasonable compensation for the provider, but the process you are using works against you. Attempts to bypass this problem often result in the provider sharing in the value added, which costs the organization significantly more than fair compensation.

The Solution - It may sound like more work, but the best way to utilize outside expertise is to seek out the best, most reputable providers and establish good relationships with them. Invite them in to assess your needs and propose results-oriented solutions. Don't try to fix everything at once, but progress in bite-sized projects. In a recent meeting I offered some innovative solutions to a long-term client. The CEO of the organization said to me, "I keep forgetting you are not one of our executives!" That is the kind of relationship that adds value to both parties over years of good relations and successful improvements. And it did NOT start with an RFP!

Key Points:

- Leaders of safety programs will begin to view the worker as the customer, analyze what is needed to work safely, try to convince the worker of the value of the safety program, and encourage true engagement in the program. Such efforts will recognize the need for buy-in, not just understanding.

- Off-the-shelf safety training will either fade away or become customizable to the specific industries and sites utilizing it. Even generic technical training will include examples realistic to the work performed by those receiving the training.

- Larger organizations with training departments and/or corporate universities will utilize consultants to develop training and onboarding programs specific to the safety strategies and needs of the organization.

- Licensing and royalty fees will be viewed with new levels of skepticism.

- RFPs will decrease in use as more companies move towards fit-for-purpose projects.

Prediction #7: Safety Metrics Will Focus on Value

- Measurements will evolve from lagging, to leading, to transformational indicators.
- Organizations will begin to use metrics to understand, rather than to react, and thus reduce measurement dysfunction in safety.
- Visions of safety success will drive metrics to measure progress toward success rather than diminishing failure rates.
- Although safety will eventually be measured by a balanced-scorecard approach, that will not happen in most organizations during the next decade.

Safety Measurement: Boring, Uninspiring, and Fear-Inducing

What excites and inspires you? Probably the first thing that entered your mind was not safety measurement. Why is something this important perceived as such a boring topic, and why does it create so much fear?

The purpose of safety measurement is to focus and align behaviors, initiatives and processes and, most importantly, to excite people about safety and the important role it plays in work. Yet many organizations do a poor job at selling its importance and demonstrating measurable positive progress towards the right goals. Based on my experience with enhancing executive measurement systems, we offer some simple questions designed to prompt internal conversations to better your measurement systems.

Question 1: What would your goals look like if they were stated in the positive? Surprisingly, even now, some of the best safety-performing organizations state their goals incorrectly. They define the desirable end-state in safety as having fewer or zero injuries, incidents or hurt people. Goals need to be positively defined if we want to inspire excitement around achieving it. Incidents are failures in your system.

Question 2: Do you want employees to fail less or succeed at accomplishing something? No one of sound mind designs their safety management systems to expect incidents. Similarly, in quality, we do not design our processes to expect defects. If or when they occur, they are failures. When we define our goals as having fewer failures, we send the message, "Work harder this year to fail less." Goals need to be defined by what you want people to do, rather than not do. Otherwise, you will create a culture focused on avoidance, rather than one focused on achievement through effort.

Question 3: How much of your safety measurement communication is focused on what you don't want, compared to what you do? In my experience, the vast majority of safety meetings where safety measurements or information is shared with the employee population, more attention is placed on discussing what is not wanted, rather than on what is. Consider discussing a near miss: focus just as much time discussing what kept it a near miss (and not an injury) as the time you spend discussing what occurred leading up to it.

Question 4: Can you directly correlate performance and results? While autonomy is important, there needs to be an aligned focus on performance in safety to achieve excellent results. When results are achieved, if we do not know what performance made it a reality, there will be a decreased sense of comfort in the ability to repeat year after year.

Question 5: Do you communicate more about results or the performance necessary to achieve the results? When we only measure and manage results, even the best intentioned people might use manipulation to achieve the results. Certainly the results are vital. In fact, we are all held accountable for results. However, when this is all that is discussed, we leave too much to the discretion of individuals to self-determine what is necessary to reach the results.

Question 6: How much creative input do those being measured have in the system? If we do not involve people in the determination of what, how, when, where and why we are measuring what we measure, expect a degree of fear or mistrust. If we want others to be excited about safety measurement, they need to understand the rationale and see how it benefits them personally and professionally.

If we desire enhanced performance and results, we need to change what, how and why we measure. This is not something that can be purchased from a vendor. Rather, it results from difficult and collaborative internal conversations. If we continue to fail to do this, safety measurement will continue to be boring, uninspiring and fear-inducing.

Safety Measurement: Culture Shaping or Failure Avoidance?

Let's take this a bit further. It is a new month. I want you all to work very hard to fail less than previous months. I'll be measuring. Failures will not be tolerated. Anyone caught doing so will be disciplined by their peers and/or leadership.

Leading and measuring with the aforementioned approach creates malicious compliance, avoidance behavior, a have-to mentality and disdain toward the organization. Teamwork becomes a pointless buzzword and fear of measurement sets in. When organizations measure only incidents, and establish and reward incident reduction goals, "fail less" becomes the message. Are your safety measurement systems focusing on motivation and excitement, or evaluation and reactive accountability?

Lagging Indicators Create Hope

Incident metrics are prescriptive when there is a lot of data. As safety improves, the data used to advance results loses statistical significance which leads to a multitude of random data points. As an organization matures in their safety management systems and culture, injury data moves from prescriptive to descriptive, then to demotivating and borderline pointless. When you achieve zero incidents, how do you continue to improve? Most importantly, are the results due to purposeful initiatives and accountability, or luck? What sense of comfort does the organization have that results will repeat next year?

An injury or incident is a failure in your prevention process. When the strategy or measurements are focusing on reducing injuries, the culture is being motivated to avoid failure rather than achieve success.

When a failure occurs and tactics are deployed quickly to prevent recurrence, there is an impression that "Leadership is reactive when it comes to safety," or, "Someone has to get hurt for safety to improve." Rarely are high-performing cultures motivated by measurement of such an approach.

Measurement: Motivational or Demotivating?

Measurement is supposed to direct, align and motivate behavior. What percent of the population in your organization is motivated, or even excited, by safety measurement compared to those who are fearful of it?

84

Executives deploy a multitude of measurement systems to validate the health of operations. Safety is no different than any other operational priority, yet few leverage balanced scorecards or transformational measurement dashboards. If safety is such an important priority or core value, how balanced and comparative are the average measurements?

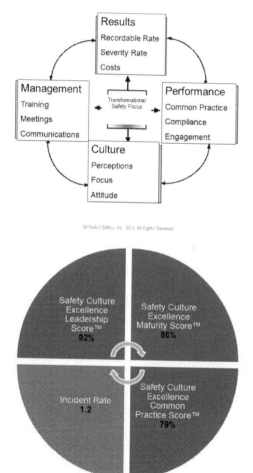

Of course, measuring results is important; ignoring this will be career-limiting. However, results alone do not identify what actions must be taken to continue achieving them. Approach a sampling of employees, tell them what the current incident rate is, and ask what they can do to impact it. How aligned are the responses with the reality of what the focus needs to be? Further, ask employees if they know how the incident rate is calculated. Unfortunately, the average reader will be disappointed by the answers they receive.

Key Questions to Identify Leading and Transformational Measurements

Working with many of the best safety-performing organizations in the industry, we have created leading, comparative indicators and overall transformational balanced scorecard safety measurement systems. Consider collaborating with other leaders and influential followers in your organization to answer the following questions. The answers to such questions can facilitate the transformation necessary for obtaining breakthrough performance.

1. What does excellence look like in behavioral terms? What would you see or hear the average employee, supervisor, manager or executive doing or saying that creates a sense of comfort that success is near, because you are effectively working your plan and executing against your strategy? If safety excellence is defined in behavioral terms (what people need to do to create the results), it is observable. If it is observable, feedback is possible. When this happens, the organization is effectively coaching for performance, rather than managing results through a trial-and-error strategy.

2. How desirable are the beliefs in the organization? Beliefs influence decisions, behaviors and stories told throughout the organization. Desirable perceptions are

a common leading indicator opportunity in the industry and measuring those through a perception survey is easier than many realize. What would the desirable perceptions be and what is the current gap?

3. How does common practice compare to desired behaviors and experiences? What is the reality of the day-to-day activities compared to what is desired?

4. How will you market safety? Yes, market safety. Often ignored, significant value is derived by focusing on branding, positioning, voice of the customer and reinforcing the buying decisions. How will measurement systems solicit discretional effort?

5. What initiatives will support the safety excellence strategy? This should be the last question of this series. Unfortunately, the average organization deploys many great attempts to improve safety, but has difficulty demonstrating how the attempt will produce measurable progress. New initiatives need to demonstrate a measurable improvement in beliefs, decisions, behaviors and stories; not just results.

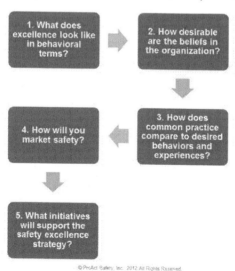

<u>Delegate Priorities, Not Values</u>
For safety to become a core value, safety improvement cannot be delegated. Values are created when, over time, beliefs are reinforced by consistent behaviors, at or near the point of decision. This requires key decision makers to be involved in the creation and continuous evolution of the measurement strategy. Measuring the right things and celebrating leading indicator progress is far too important to be the sole responsibility of the safety department if sustainable excellence is your goal.

Lagging to Leading to Transformational Indicators: Measuring the Contribution of Value

Measuring activities to determine the health of improvement efforts or culture tells you very little if excellence is your goal. Excellence is not just zero injuries or incidents; it is the ability to win through the achievement of great results, with strong and confident insight into how the results were achieved, and establishing a culture that focuses on a continuous improvement mindset.

Many well-intended organizations suffer from a programmatic focus and demonstrate an activities-based culture, whether these activities add value or not. For years, the safety profession, in particular, has tried to compete with the business goals of production by integrating activities and thinking into everything to overcome this competition. If there is no real or perceived value that is yielded by the activities, the competition continues, as it was not correctly addressed. Our strategy shouldn't be to compete; it should show how we will win by adding value. Zero injuries or incidents is the byproduct of the value of excellence, not the final goal.

Effective safety strategy, however, is still surprisingly lacking in many organizations. I have named the "strategy" in place for most organizations The Perpetual Cycle of Avoiding Failures[SM], with zero injuries being the primary, misguided goal. The cycle repeats like this: 1.) Review current injury rate. 2.) Set new injury rate or objective. 3.) Develop a list of initiatives (or programs). 4.) Execute on the efforts. 1.) Review current injury rate.

Problems arise when the rates improve. Most leaders know correlation doesn't mean causation, but this is forgotten with improved results. "We had better performance and we were doing these things; therefore, we had better performance because we were doing these things." Sounds logical, doesn't it? This is just as flawed a logic as individuals who define safe as zero injuries: "Safe means not getting hurt. So, therefore, anything I do that doesn't get me hurt must be safe!"

Alternatively, it is easy to become distracted when rates don't improve or with each new incident when the search is revived for what else can be done. More seems to be the answer or driver for improvement rather than how we do safety better. At some point, how we do safety better is answered by removing effort that is no longer value-added, even though, at one point in time, it might have been.

An effective strategy is a framework of choices an organization makes to determine how to capture and deliver value. This strategy answers, "How will we win and know we are winning?" These choices have been made by many ProAct Safety clients over the years with a culmination of advancements in what is measured. These organizations evolved from measuring lagging indicators (their results) to leading indicators (typically inputs and activities) to transformational indicators (measurement of contributed value from the activities to the results).

Consider your health as an analogy: a lagging indicator might be having or not having a heart attack. Exercise, calories burned versus consumed, and diet would be leading indicators and are comparable to how we measure our leading indicators in safety: activities and effort. If, however, you check your blood pressure and it is high or has increased, and you are making healthy eating decisions and regularly exercising, the answer is rarely more diets and increasing exercise. You might need a different intervention, as more is rarely the answer. Your blood pressure is a transformational indicator that tells you the value derived from your activities.

In both health and safety, we must all evolve to measure not just the things we do to try to improve the lagging indicator results, but also the contribution of value from our activities to our results. For safety, the following are proven examples of transformational indicators: Desired Beliefs, Emotions, Knowledge Levels, Competencies, Behaviors and Organizational Story-Telling.

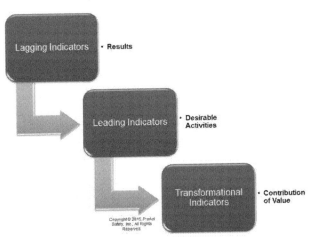

Consider training: if we only measure attendance but not whether, as a result, people know what we need them to know, believe what we need them to believe, and do or are able to do what we need them to do, is there any real return on investment of time and resources? If we had people in a class and results improved, should we trust how real and sustainable the results are?

As discussed earlier, organizations on the path towards excellence in safety performance and culture realize they need a strategy. Strategy is making trade-off choices (what will we do, not do, or stop doing) to win. As part of their strategy, the focus and measurements evolve from results and activities towards capturing and delivering value to the customers of their safety efforts. In your organization, what transformational indicators would tell you the value contributed by your safety efforts? Focus on this and you will significantly increase your chances of winning.

Key Points:

- Leading indicators will be viewed as beneficial only when they provide timely information that facilitates being proactive, preventative and predictive.

- Measurements will evolve from lagging to leading to transformational indicators that demonstrate the contribution of value from improvement efforts to results.

- Lagging measurements will play a decreased role in validating the effectiveness of the strategy, rather than drive the strategy.

- Leading and transformational measurements will be created to support the strategy.

- Organizations will mostly measure what they want, rather than what they do not want.

- Safety goals will become positive versus negative with a real vision of what safety excellence looks like, and efforts will focus on achieving success versus avoiding failure. Metrics will focus on value added to safety goals rather than exclusively on accident reduction.

- Organizations will perform a Pareto gap analysis of their performance, target specific improvement areas, accomplish the goal, celebrate success and move on to others. This will formulate the foundation of continuous improvement. Progress toward goals will provide another metric used to drive motivation and engagement.

- The two-dimensional thinking on safety metrics (leading and lagging indicators) will slowly give way to the four-dimensional thinking of the balanced scorecard (drivers, culture, performance, results).

- Measurements will prompt, direct, align and motivate behavior. Imagine that!

Conclusion

Safety efforts around the world are moving from an outsourced specialty to a mainstream business issue. Organizations no longer accept the traditional approach to safety as the best or only option. Likewise, their attraction to the academic processes and programs as complete solutions is lessening.

The direction in which we see safety going is to take a more practical, reality-based view and be addressed the same way other business issues are. All the tools of the past are still available, but leaders are more intelligently choosing which ones to use to strategically address their unique set of challenges.

In addition to the old tools, technology is providing new tools for safety. The exploration of these new tools may open up additional possibilities beyond the ones we can currently see and predict. The possibilities are growing and organizations who are serious about excellence in safety performance and culture can rise to new heights not available to the generations before.

Whether or not you agree with all our findings, exploring the trends we see from our vantage point as advisors and strategic partners with organizations of all kinds around the world can help you begin to envision your organization's unique safety future. These predictions should help you explore new possibilities and plan for and prevent potential problems that could ambush your future efforts. The future is a destination to which we are all going. The more clearly you see the destination, the better you can map your path to the specific location to which you would like to steer.

Best wishes on your journey.

Many thanks,

Shawn M. Galloway and Terry L. Mathis

The Predictions Summary

Prediction #1: Excellence Reframed – Excellence will be defined by a confidence in how great results are achieved with the mindset "we can always be better".

Prediction #2: From Programs to Strategy – Organizations will move from a programmatic to a strategic approach to safety.

Prediction #3: Leaders Actually Lead Safety – Operational leaders will take a more hands-on role in safety, supported by an increase in responsibility, clarity and behavioral accountability.

Prediction #4: Grunt to Guardian to Guru – The role of the company safety professional will be more clearly defined based on contributed value.

Prediction #5: A New Kind of Safety Consultant Will Emerge – The role of safety consultants will both change and increase in visibility.

Prediction #6: Safety Programs Will Begin to Change Their Focus – Safety programs and training will become fit-for-purpose and focus on transference of value by shifting focus from control to marketing.

Prediction #7: Safety Metrics Will Focus on Value – Measurements will evolve from lagging to leading to transformational indicators.

While the predictions above are potentially the most universal and impactful, they are certainly not the only trends we see impacting safety. There are many issues that only impact one industry or type of business. There are others that are specific to foreign countries or regions of the US. Others are largely isolated in the government sector.

The future will bring changes to all safety efforts, and those organizations and leaders who are ready for such changes will prosper while others struggle to adjust. If you would like to discuss the specific issues that will most likely impact your organization or your programs and processes, please contact ProAct Safety at info@proactsafety.com, 800-395-1347 or +1-936-273-8700.

Acknowledgements

Our sincere appreciate for the hard work of Traci Long and Lori Bowlin. Without their tireless efforts, editing, and valuable feedback, we would not have been able to accomplish this work. They remain an integral part of our consulting firm and we are honored they have decided to dedicate the past 10 years of their professional careers with us. We also thank our wives, Sara Galloway and Janie Mathis for their patience and support of our efforts, and our great clients with whom we have become true partners in safety excellence.

About the Authors

Shawn M. Galloway

Shawn is the President and Chief Operating Officer of ProAct Safety. As the leading safety culture and strategy consultant, and internationally recognized safety excellence expert, he has helped hundreds of organizations, within every major industry, achieve and sustain excellence in performance and culture. Shawn is the coauthor of two books - *STEPS to Safety Culture Excellence* (WILEY, 2013) and the *Hazardous Materials Management Desk Reference, 3rd Edition* (AHMP, 2013).

Shawn has personally worked with National Institutes of Health, Plains All American Pipeline, Crosstex Energy Services, MD Anderson, Merck, Bristol-Myers Squibb, Amway, Wrigley, Herman Miller, Eastman Chemical, Georgia-Pacific, Honda, Ingersoll-Rand, International Paper, Rockwell Automation, Timken, Starbucks, United States Capital, United States Armed Forces and over a hundred similar organizations.

National Safety Council calls him a "Global safety excellence expert" and a "Top-rated speaker" and recently listed him in the Top 40 Rising Stars of Safety. EHS Today magazine listed Shawn in The 50 People Who Most Influenced EHS, and ISHN magazine listed him in the POWER 101 – Leaders of the EHS World. Shawn has authored hundreds of podcasts, articles and videos on the subject of leadership and safety excellence in culture and performance, and is the host of the highly acclaimed weekly podcast series, Safety Culture Excellence®.

Terry L. Mathis

Terry is the founder and CEO of ProAct Safety, an international safety and performance excellence firm. He is known for his dynamic presentations and writing in the fields of behavioral and cultural safety, leadership and operational performance, and is a regular speaker at ASSE, NSC, and numerous company and industry conferences.

He is a veteran of over 1600 safety, culture and performance improvement engagements in 39 countries, and has personally assisted organizations such as Georgia-Pacific, Williams Gas Pipeline, US Pipeline, Herman Miller, AstraZeneca, Wrigley, ALCOA, Merck, Rockwell Automation, AMCOL International, Ingersoll-Rand, The United States Armed Forces and many others to achieve excellence. Terry has been a frequent contributor to industry magazines for over 15 years and is the coauthor of *STEPS to Safety Culture Excellence* (WILEY, 2013) and *Developing a Safety Culture: Successfully Involving the Entire Organization* (J.J. Keller & Associates, Inc., 1996).

EHS Today has listed Terry four consecutive times as one of The 50 People Who Most Influenced EHS. In addition to the two books, Terry has authored more than 80 articles and spoken at hundreds of private and public events.

Bibliography

Anderson, C. (2012). *Makers: The New Industrial Revolution.* New York, NY: Crown Business.

Campbell, A., Kunisch, S., & Muller-Stewens, G. (2012, Spring). Are CEOs Getting the Best From Corporate Functions? *MIT Sloan Management Review.*

Covey, S. R. (1989). *The 7 Habits of Highly Effective People.* New York: Free Press.

Galloway, S. M. (2011, February). For Sustainable Safety, Leaders Must Do More Coaching, Less Policing. *Drilling Contractor.*

Galloway, S. M. (2012, February). Safety Measurement: Boring, Uninspiring and Fear-Inducing. *BIC.*

Galloway, S. M. (2012, August). Safety Measurement: Culture Shaping or Failure Avoidance? *POWER Magazine.*

Galloway, S. M. (2013, December). Five Vital Questions to Effectively Develop Leaders. *Occupational Health & Safety.*

Galloway, S. M. (2013, September). Licensing and Royalty Fees Can Blunt Safety Advances. *ISHN.*

Galloway, S. M. (2013, August). Safety Strategy: Is Your Safety Professional a Grunt or Guru? *BIC.*

Galloway, S. M. (2013, August). Who Should Develop Corporate Safety Strategy? *Occupational Health & Safety.*

Galloway, S. M. (2013, June). You Need to Manage Strategically. *ISHN.*

Galloway, S. M. (2014, November). Finding Support: From Reducing Costs to Adding Value. *BIC.*

Galloway, S. M. (2014, September). Safety Must Deliver More Than Customers Expect. *ISHN*.

Galloway, S. M. (2014, August). The Mindset of Safety Excellence. *BIC*.

Galloway, S. M. (2014, February 4). When Leaders Don't Lead, Followers Won't Follow. *Podcast: Safety Culture Excellence*.

Galloway, S. M. (2015, March). Lagging to Leading to Transformational Indicators: Measuring the Contribution of Value. *Occupational Health & Safety*.

Galloway, S. M. (2015, January). The Only Way Safety Will Continuously Improve. *Occupational Health & Safety*.

Katzenbach, J., & Aguirre, D. (2013, Summer). Culture and the Chief Executive. *Strategy & Business*.

Kiechel, W. (2010). *The Lords of Strategy: The Secret Intellectual History of the New Corporate World*. Cambridge, MA: Harvard Business School Press.

Kofman, F. (2013, April 23). My Best Mistake: How Not to Change a Culture. *Pulse (LinkedIn)*.

Mathis, T. L. (2012, June). The Futility of RFPs. *Industry Week*.

Mathis, T. L. (2013, September 18). More is Not Better; Only Better is Better. *Podcast: Safety Culture Excellence*.

Mathis, T. L. (2013, May). Should the Safety Department Manage Safety? *Industry Week*.

Mathis, T. L. (2013, July). The Ideal Safety Career Path. *EHS Today*.

Mathis, T. L. (2014, December 17). Checking Off the Box. *Podcast: Safety Culture Excellence*.

Mathis, T. L. (2014, February). Consultants vs. Culture: Can the Two Work Against Each Other? *The Adviser*.

Mathis, T. L. (2014, February 26). Improving Safety: Programs vs. People. *Podcast: Safety Culture Excellence.*

Mathis, T. L. (2015, March). Safety Culture and Social Media. *EHS Today.*

Mathis, T. L., & Galloway, S. M. (2013). *STEPS to Safety Culture Excellence.* Hoboken, NJ: John Wiley & Sons, Inc.

Pink, D. H. (2012). Retrieved from http://www.danpink.com/resource/flip-manifesto/

† Some articles may be edited from the original published version.

For more information on how to leverage the expertise of Shawn and Terry, visit www.ProActSafety.com

"A company cannot be great without having a great safety culture. This book allows us to 'see the future of safety' and take steps to make sure we are ahead of the pack."
Paul Walsh, President & COO, Ascent Tooling Group

"I had the honor of reviewing STEPS to Safety Culture Excellence by Shawn and Terry prior to its release and found I had to read it twice just to fully grasp the astounding knowledge and expertise that was between the covers. In reviewing their latest collaboration, Forecasting Tomorrow: The Future of Safety Excellence, I am once again amazed and impressed. This is a book that all levels of management MUST read. To bring the major shift necessary in many safety programs/philosophies/cultures it is imperative that those managing the companies must think with strategic priorities and possibilities and have set plans for specific periods of time. This book is an insight as to the true future that can await us in our pursuits toward safety excellence. When I find that I can't stop re-reading the material, I know I've found a winner. This book is a homerun! I strongly recommend, no, encourage, all those who manage, or hope to manage, successful safety teams read this book."
Dennis Leonard, Safety director, Kiewit Mining Group Inc.

"This book is a great companion to STEPS to Safety Culture Excellence. Both books challenge the status quo of safety and challenge the reader to rethink traditional safety 'knowledge.' Where STEPS laid out what the journey to safety excellence might look like, this book describes what you might see along the way. For years, safety professionals have pushed for the elevation of safety within an organization. Now that safety has gotten the attention of senior company leaders, safety professionals are pushed to show value to the organization and alignment with their organization's strategy... not in an altruistic way but in a real-world, business way. This requires a change in mindset for executive, operational and safety leaders. How do we continue moving our thinking from 'Zero' to excellence. In addition to the strategic elements of safety, this book also discusses how safety programs, metrics and technology will need to be integrated into business strategies for organizational success as well as furthering safety excellence. It also challenges the current roles of safety professionals and consultants and looks at

how they might provide more business value in the future. While there may still not be a silver bullet, Shawn and Terry have found 'the yellow brick road' toward safety excellence and are enthusiastic guides."
Kelvin Roth, Director Corporate Environmental Health & Safety, CF Industries

"Once again, I compliment both Shawn and Terry for their dedication to continue to challenge our way of thinking as it relates to safety as well as how we approach safety excellence within a business culture. As an EHS professional in the Oil & Gas Industry, [I think] this book has done an excellent job forecasting trends as well as provoking new thoughts around the advancement of Safety Excellence which I have been able to apply directly to our organizational strategy. I encourage functional and operational leaders as well as EHS professionals alike who have a desire to further develop the effectiveness of their safety culture within their organization to read this book and apply its principles."
Sean Atkins, Vice President - Environmental Health & Safety, Enlink Midstream

"All of the predictions ring true and are helpful in preparing us for heading that direction. It is good thought provoking information that should be required reading for management prep. Leaders and safety professionals who read this book will have an opportunity to set themselves up to be on the leading edge of safety excellence as this movement unfolds."
Leslie Kantor, Safety Manager, NW Natural

"Forecasting Tomorrow provides an in depth look at how the field of safety is progressing beyond traditional safety management approaches. This book is a must read for any safety professional that wants to continue to adapt to the changing environment we support. Shawn and Terry provide great insight into the value in aligning and integrating safety into business in a very practical manner. Thanks Terry and Shawn for another great reference for safety and business professionals alike!"
Cory Beliveau, Manager Health & Saftey, ARC Resources Ltd.

"What a thought provoking read! I love the positive connection that Shawn and Terry make between production and safety: neither have to come at the cost of the other, but actually enhance one another. Great read! Terry and Shawn are spot on if organizations adopt Transformational Measurement into their measurement equation. It would take companies to new level of focus."
Brian Scott, President, CoreCulture

"This is a sensational book which every forward-thinking leader should read. I love the author's message that safety should have a strategic approach that focuses on value, rather than the old-school mentality of MORE programs. Take their advice to heart and you'll truly be achieving success, rather than avoiding failure."
Greg Ford, CEO, TalentClick

"Peter Drucker once famously said that 'Culture eats strategy for breakfast.' No amount of procedure or technology - the other two legs of a comprehensive safety program - can overcome a poor safety culture. Forecasting Tomorrow predicts a near-term future influenced by transparency and reputation, driven by social media and responsibility. A future where safety moves from tactics oddly separated from business strategy and policed by 'safety cops,' to a competitive advantage led with commitment throughout an organization. A future where safety is no longer regarded as a cost, but an investment - a core value recognized by management, workers, shareholders, and customers alike. Forecasting Tomorrow is a great read for those willing to take on the mantle of safety leadership in the coming years."
Steve Ludwig, Program Manager - Safety, Rockwell Automation Inc.

"Shawn and Terry's book elevates the critical goal of Safety Excellence from a risk management initiative to a key driver for Operations and Business Excellence. Oil and Gas, manufacturing, and mining organizations and consultants will find game-changing insights here."
Katherine Molly, Principal, Northland High

"I think the book is excellent and challenges many currently held convictions about safety excellence, such as 'zero injury' safety

programs being something to which EHS professionals and corporate leaders should aspire, perceived acceptable risks versus unnecessary risks and promoting a 'safety culture' as opposed to safety being ensconced as part of the business culture and included as part of business decision-making. Through their travels and meetings with corporate and safety leaders around the world, I think that Terry and Shawn probably have a better idea than most about the trends impacting safety and safety performance and are accurate in their predictions about the future of safety excellence, the most profound of which is the integration of safety into the business culture and the demand that metrics focus on value and not just meeting numerical goals like zero injuries (aka 'failing less'). As the old saying goes, 'If you want the same results, keep doing the same things.' But as Terry and Shawn point out in Forecasting Tomorrow, 'If we seek different results, we must ask more intelligent questions and realize today's answers will be antiquated tomorrow.' Having a strategic plan and working that plan to achieve sustainable safety excellence - rather than creating programs to achieve specific goals - is something that business leaders understand and safety leaders need to adopt. True corporate leaders should lead safety like they lead production and other aspects of the business. Shawn and Terry are right: 'Safety culture is an aspect of company culture and cannot be delegated or outsourced.'"
Sandy Smith, Editor-in-Chief, EHS Today

"Once again Terry Mathis and Shawn Galloway have provided a logical progression of thought on the importance of evolving the culture of Safety to prevention based contribution to bottom line business results. This is an important read for any executive to understand how growing a culture of Safety will deliver better results than slogans or campaigns."
Arron S. Angle, Executive Consultant

107

41707214R00064

Made in the USA
Middletown, DE
09 April 2019